WHAT PEOPLE ARE SAYING ABOUT SUSAN HART GAINES AND THIS BOOK

"Susan Hart Gaines' wisdom in self-care is hard earned. She has worked as a journalist, personal trainer, and life coach. Her life has carried her through messy and enlightening involvements with relationships, parenting, trauma, and self-doubt. *Prioritize Your Self-Care* packs all these experiences into a beautifully written memoir and guide that argues that caring for yourself is not a luxury but a necessity. Gaines tells you to care for yourself without fear of selfishness. She helps you connect with your intuition, boundaries, compassion, and need for silence and stillness. Her book can lead you to honor your true self."

— Jack El-Hai, Author of *The Nazi and the Psychiatrist* and *The Lobotomist*

"Forget 'luxury,' 'self-indulgent,' and 'selfish.' Coaching conversations with Susan brought reassurance, clarity, and compassion to defining self-care. And importantly, how to make self-care actionable! Susan is clear: Self-care is not a 'nice-to-have'; it's the essence of a flourishing life."

— Jenny Grew, MD

"Susan has an innate gift for being an empathetic listener. You will feel seen and understood while working with her. She has a keen ability for 'connecting the dots' and helping you see your life from a new and mindful perspective."

— Margi Heie, PT, DPT, OCS

"Imagine yourself in a journey in a strange, foreign place, attempting to understand the where, what, and how of your experience. Now imagine a walking partner who helps you reimagine the reality of where you are and where you might be going, gently asking all the questions you couldn't quite articulate, in whose answers you begin to see a different order in the universe, one you could not envision yourself. That has been my coaching experience with Susan Gaines. We're still walking, still talking, still discovering together."

— Nathan Kemalyan, MD

"Susan has a method where she takes you from stress to a place of comfort. Susan is an amazing coach and instructor. She is engaging, thoughtful, and intuitive. She uses her knowledge and abilities in her coaching so that her clients don't just learn. They feel it, see it, and then make it their own. If you wish to explore your physical, soulful, and emotional self more deeply, there is no better place, no better art, and no better coach than Susan."

— Ron Tarrel, DO

"I have never seen a written piece so cogently, so compassionately, and that so clearly addresses not only the existential struggle of a physician but also by extension the family as Susan Gaines blog post 'The Difficulty in Coming Home: What Doctors and Soldiers Have in Common.' It is the first time I've read anything by a non-physician and felt really seen. Truly a poignant commentary on the meta-existence of all of those who engage in healing particularly when life and death are on the line."

— Jeevan Sekhar, MD

"Few people are as willing as Susan Gaines to share their personal story with so much vulnerability. In *Prioritize Your Self-Care*, she reveals how she found her own calm during the storms in her life, and she offers hope and practical methods for keeping our balance even when the earth is shaking all around us. If you want to heal, start here."

— Patrick Snow, Publishing Coach and International
Bestselling Author of *Creating Your Own Destiny* and
The Affluent Entrepreneur

"This heartfelt book shares with great honesty the overwhelming and even addictive craziness we feel when family members engage in dysfunctional behaviors and how we can come to terms with not being able to control or fix the people we love. Readers will discover tips and techniques for overcoming codependency and finding their own happiness amid others' chaos."

> — Tyler R. Tichelaar, PhD and Award-Winning Author of
> *The Mysteries of Marquette*

"I was on my third episode of major burnout. Susan validated that I wasn't crazy, weak, or broken. She helped me reconnect with my superpowers (empathy, connection-building), which are devalued and undermined in a metric-driven, reductionist, myopic medical system. She has helped me reconnect with my sources of strength and renewal so I can continue to be of service."

> — Jude Bornstein-Chau, MD

"Susan really meets you where you are. She sees what's possible, then comes on the journey with you. She has a brilliant way of helping her clients figure it out on their own. Over time, my mind started to open. I continue to want to get better and better and better."

> — Eric Khetia, MD

"Susan is amazing! From day one, there was a connection and understanding. Susan has helped me identify my inner negativity but, more importantly, how to intercept those negative emotions when they matter most. I am so glad I took this journey. It has truly been life changing."

> — Ryan Tomlins, MD

"A beautifully written memoir and guide that argues that caring for yourself is not a luxury, but a necessity that can lead you to honor your true self."

— Jack El-Hai, Author of *The Nazi and the Psychiatrist*, *The Lobotomist*, and other books

Prioritize Your Self-Care

Reclaiming Your Path to an Extraordinary Life

SUSAN HART GAINES

PRIORITIZE YOUR SELF-CARE
Reclaiming Your Path to an Extraordinary Life

Copyright © 2025 by Susan Hart Gaines. All rights reserved.

Published by:

Aviva Publishing
Lake Placid, NY
(518) 523-1320
www.AvivaPubs.com

All Rights Reserved. No part of this book may be used or reproduced in any manner whatsoever without the expressed written permission of the author.

Address all inquiries to:
Susan Gaines
(612) 203-9619
susan@wildhartcoaching.com

ISBN: 978-1-63618-362-6
Library of Congress Control Number: 2024922214

Editing: Superior Book Productions
Cover Design: Nicole Kristin Gabriel
Interior Book Layout: Nicole Kristin Gabriel
Author Photo: Brianne Bland

Every attempt has been made to properly source all quotes. Permission received to quote the poem of Mark Nepo.

Printed in the United States of America

First Edition

2 4 6 8 10 12

DEDICATION

To my children, who inspire my greatest joy, challenge me to face my darkest self, and practice self-care on the deepest level. I love you both in this life and beyond.

ACKNOWLEDGMENTS

Leonid Frolov, my coach, who with his kind, loving presence has brought me to understanding the essence of myself and how deeply deserving I am of radical self-care.

Patrick Snow, my book coach, who gave me an easy-to-follow structure, honored my stories, and helped me tweak them to be of the greatest service to my readers.

My editors, Tyler Tichelaar and Larry Alexander of Superior Book Productions, for their kind, careful, and precise editing. Good editing makes good writing shine.

Co-Active Training Institute (CTI) for providing me the structure, methodology, and rigor to take care of myself, while learning to care for others. CTI taught me to hold all people as naturally creative, resourceful, and whole—starting with myself.

Positive Intelligence: provided me the structure and the jumpstart in daily meditation practice. Through this program, I experienced how mindfulness changes the brain. This belief infuses my coaching practice and daily life in more ways than I thought possible.

Al-Anon, for helping me save myself so I could be the light for others when they returned from the dark.

My clients, who trust me with the messiness of becoming self-aware and take me on their most intimate journeys into the self, for showing me the myriad forms self-care takes and demonstrating the magical possibility of transformation. They are living proof that co-active coaching works.

My friends, who demonstrate the myriad forms self-care takes; sometimes it means just staying home.

Craig, my partner in all ways, who learns right along with me what it means to take care of us, while we also take care of ourselves. His courage and commitment to our "designed alliance" is inspiring.

To my first husband. We struggled and grew. I am grateful for our lifelong friendship and our beautiful family.

For every experience I've ever had, good and bad—especially the bad. It is in the struggle to control, the letting go, that I am reminded again and again to take care of myself.

CONTENTS

Introduction:	Knowing You're Worthy	14
Chapter 1	Transforming Your Trauma	25
Chapter 2	Discovering the Leader Within	39
Chapter 3	Surrendering to Your Wilderness	53
Chapter 4	Trusting Your Intuition	69
Chapter 5	Turning Judgment Into Compassion	97
Chapter 6	Losing Yourself	113
Chapter 7	Becoming a Warrior of the Heart	127
Chapter 8	Listening for Your Angels	143
Chapter 9	Relinquishing Your Power	165
Chapter 10	Finding Freedom	183
Chapter 11	Receiving the Gifts of Alzheimer's	201
Chapter 12	Falling in Love With Yourself	219
Chapter 13	Designing Your Relationship	245
Chapter 14	Breathing Through Pandemonium	259
A Final Note	Manifesting Your Best Self	271
About the Author		277
Susan Hart Gaines Speaking and Coaching		281

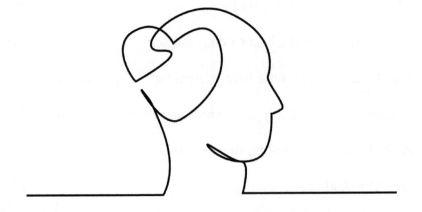

INTRODUCTION

KNOWING YOU'RE WORTHY

"To love oneself is the beginning of a lifelong romance."

— Oscar Wilde

Everybody asks for your help. You're worn out. But you can rest when you're dead. Your body aches. And not from working out. You know self-care is important, but you just don't have the time.

Does this sound like you?

I often hear these lies from my coaching clients:

- "Self-care is for the weak or wealthy."
- "Self-care is a great idea. I'd love to take a bubble bath and wash all my troubles away!"

- "Wouldn't that be nice to go to a spa! But who has that kind of money or time?"
- "I'm too busy taking care of others to take care of myself. Maybe when I retire."
- "I feel guilty when I do things for myself!"
- "Self-care is selfish; it's contrary to a life of service."

Do any of these sound like you?

While self-care is a high value for many, few of us practice it. And, when we do, we feel guilty, as Birchbox.com, a beauty products website, found in their comprehensive study on self-care:

- 67 percent of people report caring for others over their own self-care
- 33 percent of people feel guilty taking time for themselves
- 43 percent of single people make time for their self-care
- 30 percent of people in relationships make time for self-care
- 51 percent of Americans feel burned out
- 30 percent of Americans are making time for self-care

Are you feeling burned out or just run down? Have you lost your mojo? Are you putting your relationships with your significant other, children, or others ahead of yourself? Are you kicking the self-care can down the road?

I've been there. The first time I heard "Take care of yourself" was in 1989. My husband James[1] and I lived in the desert of New Mexico. We had one car, no friends, and families that lived far away. We had very little money, and as a medical resident, James was rarely home. My tiny newborn son, Ian, seemed to be uncomfortable in his own skin from the moment he was pulled from my womb by emergency C-section. He took only catnaps and cried for stretches far beyond the descriptive "witching hour." A deep ache still plagued me in the form of a half-smile scar along the top of my pubic bone—a constant reminder that even in the immediate aftermath of childbirth, I was alone.

My marriage was already hanging by a thread when, one weekend, the hospital where James was supposed to be moonlighting told me they'd never heard of him. My stomach in knots, I'd started rifling through his pockets when I found a neatly folded sexy shirtless caricature of him, drawn by an unknown artist who simply signed the work "MC." Questioning my most basic reality, I called the marriage therapist we had seen once or twice, hoping she'd talk me out of my fears: *What if he's an imposter? What if he isn't even a doctor? What if he's having an affair?* She listened compassionately, but, of course, she did not know enough to honestly, responsibly put me at ease.

So, she said the phrase that has been rattling around in my brain ever since: "Take care of yourself, Susan."

---

1 Throughout, I've changed the names of most people, including my spouses and children, to protect their privacy. This is my story, not theirs.

At first, those words, "Take care of yourself," sounded dismissive and even insulting. It was like sending a "get well soon" card to someone who is terminally ill. "How am I supposed to take care of myself," I raged, after hanging up. "Take a bubble bath? Light some candles?" I was isolated, lonely, exhausted, often in pain, and full of self-recrimination. "How is a walk in the park or a bath going to fix all this?"

Sure, weekly massages, IV vitamin drips, hyperbaric oxygen chambers, lymphatic compression suits, cryotherapy, red-light beds, and other cash-only complimentary wellness treatments can certainly help us feel better. But the idea that these things will fix you—*if* you can afford to buy them—is one of many get-happy-quick lies. Self-care, defined only as costly services, keeps the deeper pursuit of self-care out of reach for many ordinary folks. The promise that you can somehow buy your way to self-care only serves to keep us depleted and stuck in pain.

So, what does self-care really mean? It took me the next several years and many more hardships to discover the deeper meaning of self-care. Only in the rearview mirror of my life could I see that by bushwacking my way through uncharted territory did I find the way to my extraordinary life. Only later could I see that my worst times were my greatest gifts, paving the way for authentic self-care. This was not a path of bubble baths and candles. It was a survival course.

Here I am, more than thirty years later, echoing the same advice that therapist gave me: Take care of yourself. Self-care is *not* a luxury only for the wealthy. Self-care is our birthright. Babies do it naturally. They sleep when they're tired, they exercise as part of life, their posture is perfect, they cry when they're sad, they ask for what they need. As we grow and learn to balance our needs with others, self-care must be retrieved, reclaimed. Because self-care is no less foundational than it was when we were babies.

In this book, I offer my stories in the hope that in them you will see yourself and feel less alone. From my struggles, self-inquiries and, ultimately, strategies emerged. If you try my tips and self-discovery questions, you will learn to prioritize your self-care. With my Five Wellness Strategies, you will learn to prioritize your self-care so you can live your birthright of an extraordinary life:

1. Set healthy boundaries.
2. Monitor and marshal your energy sources.
3. Create pockets of silence and stillness so you can…
4. Learn the language of your body.
5. Listen to all of yourself: body, heart, mind, spirit, and emotion.

This book is both a memoir and guide. My advice is born of experience. Through accounts of my own heartbreaks and traumas, from being alone in the wilderness to an emergency C-section and visiting my son in jail, together we'll discover what self-care can mean for *you* so you can come home to your own truth and live a life of authentic purpose. I recommend you use this book as a kindred spirit, a co-explorer, with the goal of finding unconditional and loyal friendship with yourself. Only in self-compassion can you ultimately live the life of greatest possibility.

This is not a cry for soft-and-fuzzy, feel-good treatments. This is a book for self-care warriors. In that spirit, I challenge you to make self-care a top priority. This is the path to living an extraordinary life—as you define extraordinary. Throughout this book, I will provide opportunities to reflect on your own experiences and show you how to use them to light the way to your own self-care plan. It must be your own journey. Learning to take care of yourself is the ultimate personal journey. After all, self-care is an inside job.

You may be asking: Who is this self-care expert?

My seemingly disparate educational paths have all come together in this book. I am a Professional Certified Life Coach (PCC) with the International Coaching Federation (ICF) and a proud graduate of the Coactive® Training Institute (CTI). These certifications, however, do not tell the story that got me there. Before becoming a life coach, I was coaching people toward their deepest and most authentic selves through the mind-body exercise of the Gyrotonic® and Gyrokinesis® methodologies.

These separate but related exercise systems share principles with tai chi, swimming, yoga, and dance. Gyrotonic uses a weighted pulley system; the equipment helps people create space in the joints and length in the muscles. Gyrokinesis is usually taught in a class format, using only stools and mats. It is choreographed to move practitioners through nearly every joint in the body in a single hour-long session. Because it is gentle, rhythmic, and related to one's breath, the movements are the essence of mind-body exercises.

Through these deeply healing, connecting modalities, I first healed my own trauma and learned to love myself. My passion to share this life-giving movement with others led me to become an accidental entrepreneur. I say "accidental" because I did not set out to run a business. I simply wanted to share the expansive exercise system with others. My passion led me to open one of the largest Gyrotonic/Gyrokinesis studios in the Twin Cities and ultimately name it Embody Minneapolis.

I also have a Master of Science in Journalism from Northwestern University. My training as a reporter has given me essential tools for researching and writing inspirationally about my passions. I am and have always been a communicator. Little did I know that one day my passion for communication, my deep empathy, and my dedication to helping others take care of themselves would culminate in a second entrepreneurial business. With Wild Hart Coaching, I help people connect to their deepest power by finding friendship with themselves so they can achieve extraordinary lives—with grace, joy, and ease.

Most importantly, I am a mother, grandmother, and humanitarian, and I have dedicated my life to being in service to others. My hope is that this book will both serve and inspire you to put yourself first and prioritize your self-care so you, too, can be of service.

I certainly don't have all the answers. While this book is not meant to be a get-Zen-quick book, you *will* find self-care tips you can use right now. Then, at the end of each chapter, I ask questions to help you reflect on your own experience, strength, and hope. This is my life coaching approach; I help you create courageous space to explore yourself so you can take on the world in ways that align with your deepest values.

You may be reading this book to pick up a couple of quick tips, and those are in this book too. You might be a single parent, laid off, or just struggling with "not good enough" or "too much." I was there. And I still have my moments. Plenty of my clients—even those who appear to have it all—struggle with feelings of inadequacy, shame, imposter syndrome, perfectionism, and burnout. Coaching helps us come home to ourselves, recognize the lies of the internal gremlins, and embrace our magnificence. I hope this book will do the same.

Are you ready to discover the deeper and life-changing meaning of self-care? Are you ready to get beyond the clichés, beyond bubble baths, and make self-care not just a luxury but a necessity? Are you ready to get out of your own way, stop wasting time with fear, and jump into a life of greater success, ease, and happiness?

Then let's go! I challenge you to stop kicking the self-care can down the road and start prioritizing it every day as though your life depended on it. Because it does. Here you will learn the radical act of paying attention to what you need—not only in times of stress—but all the time. The future is now. Self-care is about saying, "My well-being matters. I matter." Now is the time to reclaim your path to an extraordinary life. Self-care is not a luxury. It is your birthright.

Susan Hart Gaines

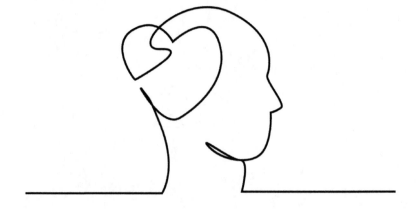

CHAPTER 1

TRANSFORMING YOUR TRAUMA

"Trauma is not what happens to us, but what we hold inside in the absence of an empathetic witness."

— Dr. Bessel van der Kolk

I had just turned seventeen, and I walked with new confidence toward College Avenue for my 10 a.m. haircut. The bay fog had already burned off, leaving a perfect spring day in Berkeley, California.

"Hi," said a man, stepping to the edge of the sidewalk in exaggerated gallantry. "How you doing today?"

He was the garbage man. He leaned on the can as though it were his pulpit.

I was vaguely aware that the truck stood idling a few houses away, waiting for him.

"Fine," I replied. I tried not to slow my gait, but I was also sure to smile so as not to seem unfriendly.

"Yeah," he said darkly. "You lookin' fine."

A chill went through me as I passed him. I tried to ignore the fear that made the back of my neck prickle as I felt his hard eyes on my backside. The huge trees were still, creating an intricate lace pattern across the quivering blue sky. I was almost to the busy avenue, to my appointment.

The sidewalk grew choked with overgrown hedges, just yards from the Elmwood fire station where a few firefighters were out cleaning their truck. Then I heard him fall in behind me. His footsteps grew louder and faster, almost running toward me.

I fought every instinct to turn around to look. I'm not sure why I didn't turn to see who was coming. Or what difference that moment would have made. Maybe I didn't turn around because I knew the firefighters were right there, just a hundred yards away.

What could happen in a span of moments within sight of saviors?

I do know that was the last time I walked down the street without compulsively and repeatedly looking over my shoulder. The footsteps became a rustle so close behind me there was no longer room to turn-around. So, I stepped back to let the person pass me.

But he wasn't there to pass me.

His hot breath was inches from my face.

I have never been able to recall the exact words he used. It was more of an acrid, evil energy than words.

I froze. I tried to speak. But I couldn't breathe.

He ran his hands over every part of me. It could have been seconds, but the act was forever.

He said something else. A threat of sorts about what he was going to do next.

I tried to speak again. Something came out.

"Don't," I think it was. It was barely audible, though the force inside me was volcanic.

"Don't," I said again, this time louder.

With that, we both bolted like deer—him back toward his filth and me toward the bright, bustling avenue, oblivious to the fact that I was a very different girl than the one who'd left my childhood home less than ten minutes earlier.

I ran past the firefighters, who were unaware of the attack that had just happened, past their shining red truck, past the bakery, the scent of freshly baked cinnamon rolls wafting out, past Sweet Dreams where I'd spent my weekly allowance buying candy before I turned thirteen and started saving it for jeans.

I ran blindly, trying to run off the smell of garbage, until I reached the pharmacy. I went to the magazine section and stood there, trying to catch my breath, staring unseeing at the covers of *Seventeen*, *Glamour*, and *Vogue*—fresh-faced girls with feathered hair.

When I finally composed myself, I felt sick. I searched my mind for a reason why he'd chosen me to violate. At the same time, I told myself I had no reason to feel the horror I felt. "At least he didn't rape me."

Those were the words I used to minimize my trauma and gaslight myself until I was in therapy thirty years later. I didn't tell anyone because, surely, it was my fault.

From then on, I wore my mother's baggy clothes and a sun visor, and I vowed not to say hello or smile.

But as it turned out, smiling or not smiling, saying hi or not saying hi, made no difference.

Later that summer, while I walked along a fire trail in the Berkeley Hills, a runner, a man who appeared to be in his thirties, said hello as he ran by. I did not speak or look at him and continued walking. He continued running, and without slowing his stride, spewed "bitch." He continued his verbal attack without even slowing his pace and then threatened to rape me in such vile words that I felt as though I'd been physically attacked.

When it came time to turn around and head back to my car, I was terrified. With every bend in the trail, I anticipated him jumping out and attacking me. The greatest terror of all was my memory of being unable to scream, let alone fight just months before.

I made it back to my car, untouched. But this time, I didn't blame myself. I wanted to kill him.

I drove all over the Berkeley Hills looking for him. I wanted to look him in the eye, tell him he had ruined my walks for years, and then run him over. In fact, I would never walk or run that trail again. It would be years before I felt safe enough to walk in nature by myself.

Fortunately for him—and for me—I never found him.

I considered shaving my head and told my anti-war-protesting father I wanted to buy a gun. No one in Berkeley owned a gun. My posture changed; my shoulders rolled forward.

By the time I got to college a few months later, I was eighteen and already worn out from all my vigilance and hatred. Before I even declared a major, I found a Tae Kwon Do class and began training. I wanted to protect myself. No, it was more than that. I wanted to dominate. I wanted to terrify. I wanted to be untouchable. One kick, one punch at a time, I began to organize and channel my fury and fear. But I also wanted to reclaim my power and dignity. The first time I landed a kick on my teacher's face, I apologized profusely, shocked that I'd hit the mark. His eyes were sparkling, like he'd just seen a rare gem. "That. Was. Beautiful," he said. "Never apologize for that."

For the next twenty-four years, I practiced and taught the Korean martial art, achieving a third-degree black belt. Through commitment to its discipline, I began to reclaim my power and dignity. Through the art of kicking and punching, I became my own firefighter, able to look men in the eye as they passed me on the sidewalk. But mostly, I just trusted myself and crossed the street, always vigilant of men who might attack me.

No matter how strong I got, how many boards I could break, for many years, my shoulders still inexplicably rolled forward, protecting my heart and the flesh that covered it. I still occasionally dream of firefighters. In my dreams, they save me.

WHAT I LEARNED

Trauma is not what happens, but the story we tell ourselves about it. I was alone and young. But sexual trauma knows no bounds; it affects people of all ages, ethnicities, genders, and levels of education.

As with many victims of sexual violence, I blamed myself. In the absence of an empathic witness, this self-blame grew from a wound to a deep, hidden injury I carried with me for many years.

My frequent denial tactic was to tell myself, "I wasn't raped. I didn't have it so bad." This minimizing prolonged the pain. It would be years before I went to therapy. And even longer before I acknowledged what happened to me that day was trauma. You don't have to wait that long.

Through embracing the evolving women's movement, martial arts practice, therapy, coaching, meditation, prayer, and writing, I eventually released the pain, fear, and rage to heal.

Not everyone has experienced trauma or recognizes what they have experienced as such. Some have experienced much worse. We all lost our innocence at some point. And we have all had times when we've felt blissfully, gratefully alive. Gratitude and loss of innocence are often two sides of the same coin. Being able to tap into both is the key to being awake to your life—both its challenges and its beauty.

SELF-CARE DISCOVERY EXERCISES

1. Recall the first time you lost your innocence. Write about it.

   _____
   _____
   _____
   _____
   _____
   _____
   _____

2. Recall the first time you reclaimed your innocence. How did you do that?

   _____
   _____
   _____
   _____
   _____
   _____
   _____

3. How has trauma affected your spiritual beliefs? Did these experiences deepen or dull your spiritual connection?

　

4. How do you call on surviving these experiences in challenging times? If you don't, how might you going forward?

5. Who are your firefighters—those who've stood up for you, believed in you, or been your empathic witnesses?

_____

_____

_____

_____

_____

_____

_____

_____

TIPS FOR TRANSFORMING YOUR TRAUMA

1. Trust your gut—and the hair on the back of your neck when it stands up.

2. Develop the practice of being in your body.

3. Learn to believe: People's mistreatment of you is not your fault.

4. Practice gratitude: What did your trauma teach you?

SUMMARY

> "Healing is never complete until we have been truly heard. May the universe send you someone who will sincerely care to listen."
>
> — Anthon St. Maarten

It took me many years to name my experience "trauma." When I finally went to therapy, it wasn't for me; it was family therapy, ostensibly to help my teenage son. One day, my family didn't show up. As I sat alone in the waiting room, the therapist came out, looked around, and said, "Well, I guess it's just you today."

So began the peeling back of the onion of my wounds and triumphs. When I finally touched on the story of the garbage man, I tried to minimize it, as I always had. "At least I wasn't raped," I said. My therapist didn't fall for my ruse.

"It's not about what other people have experienced," she said. "Please, Susan, can you just spend a few minutes feeling the pain of what happened?"

I trusted her, so I did. That was the beginning of healing. My therapist was my empathic witness for this event and others, too. I challenge you to find an empathic witness in a therapist or coach—someone who will see and hear you completely. I challenge you to stand up for yourself by being kind to yourself first.

And I challenge you to stop blaming yourself. You did the best you could with what you knew at the time. I challenge you to call garbage by its name. Just because garbage touched you does not make you garbage. I challenge you to stand up and fight—even if it's many years later—for yourself. Because you matter.

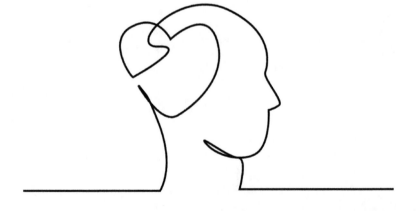

CHAPTER 2

DISCOVERING THE LEADER WITHIN

"I now walk into the wild."

— Jon Krakauer

Have you ever found yourself utterly alone? Have you ever had to rely only on yourself, without another human soul in sight? I was seventeen, two weeks into a survival course in the Sierra Nevada wilderness, when the patrol leaders dropped us off at our solo sites.

The three-day solo experience was modeled after a Native American vision quest—a coming-of-age test reserved mostly for adolescent males. I rolled my eyes at the woo-woo appropriation of a Native American ritual. But I was uneasy. At first, I tried to mask my anxiety about being left alone in the wilderness without food, telling myself it was a well-deserved break from the constant physical exertion. We'd been moving every day for almost two weeks, covering some 150 miles of rugged terrain, only stopping for more than a day when we set up a base camp for rock climbing.

I was looking forward to letting my backpack sit for a while—it was so heavy my right arm had grown numb, tingly, and weak. I could no longer count on it to hold me up or even to hold a cup without it suddenly giving out. I'd finally get to rest, I told myself, and not have to listen to my patrol mate Rachel's whimpering and moaning with each step as her brand-new hiking boots rubbed against her blistered heels.

But danger tugged at the edges of my relief. The patrol leaders had warned us the biggest killers in the wilderness were hypothermia, burns, and infections (from something as small as a blister). This lunar landscape above the timberline was where the Donner Party had infamously tried to escape the disease-ridden Midwest and move on to the land of milk and honey. Many had died, turning on each other, some even cannibalizing family members to survive. Like many Californians, I'd been raised on the cautionary tale of humans losing their humanity to survive.

Though it was not winter, I was well aware of how quickly a mild day could turn deadly. The wilderness was not fair, but it was just.

My favorite patrol leader, Sally, walked me to my site. She moved like a deer. With brown hair, brown eyes, and brown boots, she was gentle and sure in her step as she instructed me not to wander or forage for food. This wasn't about finding my own food, she reminded me. This was about fasting and facing myself. Each day, I was to build a cairn, a small rock tower, atop a granite boulder to let the leaders know, at least for the moment, I was safe. They would, in turn, knock it down to let me know they'd been there and seen it. This small act proved to be essential to my sanity and the only proof I was still part of the human tribe.

Sally showed me a little clear pond for drinking and then said goodbye, walking away. I turned my back quickly to hide my fear and faced the austere landscape some 11,000 feet above sea level. No trees grew here. I stood there, weighing barely 100 pounds, at once the tallest thing around and infinitesimal against the sky.

I had a journal, pen, tarp, and sleeping bag. I did not waste time using these things to stave off the inevitable: being alone with myself.

I strung my tarp between boulders, anchoring the edges with sticks and stones, trying to angle it just right in case it rained. Hypothermia came from getting wet, being unable to dry off, and growing cold. This was in 1978, pre-Smart Wool and technical fibers. I angled and re-angled, until I was sure any water would roll off and away from my sleeping bag. The project took no more than an hour. The rest of the day yawned before me, a massive expanse of time that felt as boundless as the wilderness.

Next, I wrote. I wrote and wrote and wrote. Lists of what and whom I missed. My boyfriend, a first love who had made me cry far more often than he had made me smile. But I was addicted to him. I made lists of all the details of my bedroom, reconstructing my life in vivid detail. I wrote everything I could think of until I was bored with the sound of my own adolescent thoughts. For hours, I disappeared into the pages of my journal, creating scenes that took me away from the emptiness of the landscape and my gnawing hunger.

I wrote until I had nothing else to say. I'd emptied myself of every word and memory. I closed my journal and sat on a granite slab, warm from the sun. The sky was clear blue, quivering in its clarity. The scene was filled with silence except for the wind rushing through the trees in the ravine far below.

I hadn't eaten in two days. I had one more to go.

As my mind emptied, small, puffy clouds gathered in the sky.

If it rains, I'll get wet, be unable to dry off, get hypothermia, and die. Now I was not only starving, but I was scared.

Hush, the wind in the trees far below said. *Hush.*

The sound of the wind blowing through the trees shushed up from below. The clouds thickened and darkened a bit, but they were still far away.

Thunder rumbled.

My heart beat faster.

I knew fear was my greatest enemy. So, I made up a little Winnie-the-Pooh-like poem for this occasion.

It's nice to know
that if it rains
I'll be okay.

I'd been afraid to speak aloud, telling myself it would be a sign I'd lost my mind. But something inside me told me perhaps the sound of my own voice would actually calm me. So, I recited the little poem, rocking back and forth, my arms wrapped around my knees, to the rhythm of the words. I paused between each line until I could hear the strength and conviction in my own voice.

It was an affirmation. Each time I repeated the poem, I grew more certain it was true.

Suddenly, three deer appeared: a buck, a doe, and a fawn. I froze, holding my breath as we do when we want the moment to last forever. The doe and I locked eyes. She froze, too, taking me in with her liquid brown eyes.

I don't know what she saw in mine, but I like to think she saw one of her kind.

I held my breath.

Then a thought came to me: The deer came while I was rocking and breathing and reciting a poem, although much quieter by the time they showed up. I was soothing myself—or trying to—and they came.

I once heard that a deer knows if a mountain lion is hungry from a mile away. They did not stumble upon me. They chose me.

My poem was not only an affirmation; it was an invocation. It was as though being myself, taking care of myself, was a signal to the deer that I was safe. Though it would be another two decades before I recognized what had happened in the High Sierra Nevada wilderness that day, I believe now they answered my call.

I began to breathe again.

For the next several minutes, the deer family grazed around me. Once, the doe stopped and we locked eyes again; she poured her wild heart into mine. The clouds gathered and darkened. When the thunder clapped, the deer bounded away, heading for cover.

For a moment, I was bereft, alone again, abandoned. "Oh, please don't leave me," I said.

But then I remembered: I am the girl who called the deer. If I trust my deepest inner voice, I will always be okay.

It did not rain after all that day.

After three days, I went to the cairn, sat on the ground leaning against a rock, and waited to rejoin our human tribe. One of my patrol mates came too. He sat on the other side of the boulder and waited. He was terribly thin. He spoke for a few minutes, telling me about his home in Iran, how much he missed it, how much he missed his parents, and the delicious food of his homeland. Then there was nothing left to say. Talking was tiring, so we waited in silence, our backs against the boulder, together.

Sally came to fetch me. She came softly so as not to frighten me. At first, I could not speak. I hid my face. The sounds coming out of me were strange, a catch of joy and relief in my throat. It was as though I'd lost human language. No words came.

The rest of the patrol held back in the trees. We were brought back to the group in silence. Someone told me later in that moment that I was wild, like a deer.

WHAT I LEARNED

Since my Sierra Nevada solo experience, deer have always been my familiar. They seem to find me when I need them most, even in the middle of the city. They are a symbol of innocence and intuition. Their appearance reminds me of my resilience, sensitivity, and inherent goodness. Their trust is a sacred honor reminding me that beautiful and powerful things will come my way if I simply open my heart and listen to what the Universe is asking of me.

I belong to the mystical and wild world. I am part of the animal kingdom. God speaks through animals, and if our hearts are sincere, if we truly listen to what the world has to say, we will discover our wider belonging.

SELF-CARE DISCOVERY EXERCISES

1. Write about a time when you felt or have been totally alone.

_____
_____
_____
_____
_____
_____
_____

2. What's the difference between being alone and being lonely?

___

3. Which animal or other familiar do you connect with? How does your connection help you in challenging times?

___

4. How is facing yourself the true beginning of self-care?

_____

_____

_____

_____

_____

_____

_____

5. Recall the most challenging period or moment in your life. What special knowledge did the experience leave you with?

_____

_____

_____

_____

_____

_____

_____

6. How can you remind yourself of the leader within? (For example: I have images and figures of deer throughout my home.)

_____

_____

_____

_____

_____

_____

TIPS FOR DISCOVERING YOUR LEADER WITHIN

1. Be quiet every day. Meditate.

2. Listen to what the world and life want of you. Pray for guidance

3. Know you are perfect exactly the way you are.

4. Push yourself a bit outside of your comfort zone.

SUMMARY

"Go out in the woods, go out. If you don't go out in the woods nothing will ever happen and your life will never begin."

— Clarissa Pinkola Estes

You may not believe animals and their spirits can guide us. Or perhaps you just haven't found yours yet. But everyone has at least one superpower, born of a challenging event or period. Discovering and cultivating yours is key to living a courageous life.

I challenge you to go into the silence, literally into the woods or figuratively into your heart. I challenge you to remember who you are, what you've endured, and the gifts you carry within. I challenge you to discover your connection to what is wild and natural within yourself. I challenge you to honor yourself, take care of yourself, and call the beautiful and true into your life.

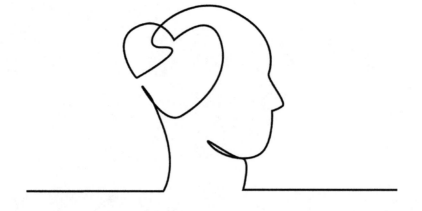

CHAPTER 3

SURRENDERING TO YOUR WILDERNESS

"Very little grows on jagged rock.
Be ground. Be crumbled, so wildflowers will come up where you are.
You've been stony for too many years.
Try something different.
Surrender."

— Rumi

When have you surrendered to uncontrollable circumstances? When has someone held your hand because it was the only thing left to do?

My first experience with surrender came with childbirth. I was twenty-seven, married five years already. When James and I were in Albuquerque for his residency, he was on call every third night. He'd get home hollowed out, his eyes dark and far away. For some reason that escapes me now, I thought this would be a good time to have a baby. He agreed. Perhaps he thought having a baby would keep me entertained and give me companionship while I waited for him to come home.

Now I could feel the amniotic fluid gushing out into the bath water. Then there was blood. Just a little bit, snaking into the water, then disappearing. With each gush of water, blood snaked out too.

"Call," I said. "I think we should call."

James went to the other room to call from our landline. I could hear him, already practiced at his calm doctor voice, trying to reassure the triage nurse more than she was apparently reassuring him. He returned to the bathroom and held up a towel for me.

"Let's go," he said. "Just in case."

The nurses looked unconcerned at first. But when I showed them the blood-tinged water that had soaked the makeshift pad I'd made to line my underwear, they grew hurried. A nurse struggled to get an internal monitor onto the baby. My cervix was not even a centimeter open. Hands shoved and groped, ending in failure.

More blood.

The nurses spoke in low, concerned voices and settled for an external monitor, which they strapped around my belly. They intently watched the lines moving up and down on the monitor, which was pushing out a paper readout of my baby's heartrate.

"Oh, there's a beat-to-beat," one nurse said, her voice relieved.

Beat-to-beat. The sound of the words calmed me.

"There," she said, "another beat-to-beat," as though she'd spotted a rabbit and took it as a sign that the predators were gone.

"Come on; let's see another," she said, trying not to sound desperate. The beat-to-beats disappeared.

"Look," a nurse said after a few minutes, drawing close to my face. "We might have to do a C-section. If we do, it's going to be an emergency. That means people are going to stop talking to you and everything is going to move very fast. If you need to have a nervous breakdown, have it now. Real fast."

I cried, a dry shaky cry, not fully grasping what was happening.

She was right. About that, I was not surprised. Everything started to move very fast. But it wasn't so much the speed, but that no one looked at me anymore that caused me consternation.

"When did you last eat? What did you eat?" they asked, prepping me for surgery.

James tried to help me as I grew mute.

I receded further and further back into my body, until I was like a little animal burrowed inside myself, watching the world rush around me.

I began to shake uncontrollably. Someone asked me if I was cold.

"Yes," I nodded. I learned later I was going into shock.

Suddenly, everything changed. I was jetted down the corridor on a gurney as though on a magic carpet. Masked surgeons flew alongside me. I was completely powerless, just a body with a mound for a stomach, bouncing down the corridor toward an unknown fate.

James was barred at the door of the operating room. They stopped him at the threshold, later explaining they didn't want him to see me intubated.

The hurried pace increased in the operating room. "Shaving," a man said, as he shaved my pubic hair off. (In the first draft, my typo read "public." Perhaps I should have left that. My hidden parts had never been so public.)

The same man suddenly dropped an instrument, which clanged as it hit the floor.

"Jesus," he said under his mask.

I suddenly had a clear thought: *I am dying. Rushing and cursing. This is what it looks like when they're trying to save a life. I must be dying.*

I turned toward the man at my left, the one who'd said, "Jesus."

"Am I dying?" I asked him.

He stopped and put his hand on my forehead. The entire room seemed to stop with him.

"Oh, no, sweetheart," he said. "We would never let you die."

"Will you just hold my hand then?" I asked.

He gripped my left hand. The nurse who'd told me to have a quick nervous breakdown reached through a wall of medical personnel and squeezed my right hand.

Far away at the door, James waved.

There are many ways to experience powerlessness. You can go down fighting, alone, humiliated, struggling—or by waving the white flag, putting your hands up, or tapping out. One way or the other, I was going to drop into darkness and knives were going to cut me open to try to save my firstborn's life. I chose surrender. In doing so, I asked for a hand and got two.

They strapped a mask over my nose and mouth, and I felt as though I was suffocating. Then everything went black.

It was the darkest place I'd ever been, darker than a windowless room. Not even a crack of light seeped in from under the door. Black as ink, void of memory. To this day, it is all I know of death. I was lucky enough to be reborn.

Coming back into the light was a journey from the center of the earth. I clawed my way up toward a voice, a sound from a distant land, a scent. Coaxing me up from unconsciousness each time I fell back in, over and over. I clawed back up from the drugged darkness into the wilderness of motherhood.

He appeared to float in the semi-darkness as an offering, or a consolation for the agony radiating through my bones. I bushwhacked through my pain toward the sensation of softness—my baby's skin—as the nurse held my baby's cheek to mine.

"Here's your baby," the nurse whispered. "Here he is."

His newborn scent was an elixir of life.

Being intubated had left my throat raw. My thirst was like a vast desert. I was only allowed ice chips, which James slipped into my mouth. Then I'd drop back into darkness.

I have no idea how long this climb toward the light and then descent into anesthetic darkness went on. But each time I returned, staying longer and longer, I was with this tiny, gurgling creature who seemed to be waiting for me, his eyes wide open as though he'd just come from another world in another body. This was not his first go-round on the planet.

"No one told me I would fall in love," I exclaimed, staring into my son Ian's tiny, alert face the next morning.

I stayed extra days in the hospital as they tried to stabilize my blood pressure and waited for my digestive system to awaken. Each time Ian cried, with excruciating pain, I twisted and lifted him out of his bassinette beside me and tried to nurse him. We'd fall asleep content as two lambs cuddled together. I'd awaken, Ian on my chest, move him back to the bassinette, again in agony, only to start the entire process over again.

A nurse I guessed to be about sixty or so came into my room in the middle of the night. "Are you getting any sleep at all, sweetheart?"

Being called sweetheart by this motherly figure brought tears to my eyes. My own mother was far away both geographically and emotionally.

"Not really," I said. I said every time I put my baby to my breast, he just fell asleep.

"He's not hungry," she said with warm wisdom. "He just wants to be next to you, to hear your heartbeat. Just keep him with you on your chest," she said.

"Can I do that?" I asked.

"Yes," she said with comforting authority. "I have never known a mother to squish her baby."

After that, Ian and I slept for hours at a time, as if he were still in my womb.

James, who was on rounds, visited us like the other patients. He'd stop in our room and put a hand on my shoulder, more like a doctor than my partner. But I had motherly nurses and an electric bed to help me for now.

When it was time to leave the hospital five days later, I was afraid to leave the cocoon of support. I knew I was going home to an empty house where I'd wait for my husband to come home at night to lift anything over ten pounds. I would soon learn the most difficult time—the time of "go-it-alone"—was yet to come.

But for now, a nurse pushed me out of the hospital in a wheelchair—another lesson in powerlessness—my tiny son Ian in my lap. It had snowed. The scent of woodsmoke filled the air. The nurse tucked us into the car James had pulled around. I tried not to cry as I said goodbye to the nurse. As my husband silently drove us toward our rented adobe, toward the Sandia Mountains sparkling with snow, I called myself sweetheart.

Sweetheart, it will be okay.

WHAT I LEARNED

"Faith is the bird that feels the light when the dawn is still dark."

— Rabindranath Tagore

Surrender is not the same as giving up or giving in. Surrender is courageous. It relies on faith, which is the absence of any guarantee, and so it is the foundation of spiritual connection. I went under the knife believing my medical team would never let me die. This belief was the difference between acceptance and struggle. So many things are beyond our control, but how we relate to those circumstances is the difference between suffering and serenity. I was scared. But by relinquishing control, I found surrender was indeed sweet.

Childbirth was my first great lesson in being powerless. Ian's traumatic birth set the stage for the lessons he continued to teach me as he grew. He was my guru of letting go. He came into the world teaching me I had no control over another human, least of all how they come into the world. Today, I've come to see motherhood at the highest level: I am my children's guide on earth, but I do not get to say how they are born—or how they live.

SELF-CARE DISCOVERY EXERCISES

1. Write about a time when you were powerless or when you had to let others carry you or your burden.

   _____
   _____
   _____
   _____
   _____
   _____
   _____
   _____
   _____
   _____
   _____
   _____

2. What did you learn? What gifts and/or opportunities did you experience?

___

3. Who helped you, the ones who held your hand or reassured you? Identify those people in your life now.

___

4. How did this experience change your perspective?

_____

_____

_____

_____

_____

_____

_____

4. What is the relationship between surrender and self-care? How is knowing when to surrender a form of self-care?

_____

_____

_____

_____

_____

_____

_____

TIPS FOR PRACTICING SURRENDER

1. Ask yourself: How important is it?

2. Listen to whatever is keeping you in the fight. Is it ego, fear of judgment, or something else? Pray for guidance.

3. Remember faith is a verb—it is something to practice and build strength in.

4. Notice where you surrender to the unknown every day.

SUMMARY

"Look for the helpers. You will always find people who are helping."

— Fred Rogers

We find great vulnerability in surrender. It is a way of saying with your body, mind, and soul, "I can't do this alone. Please help me." Surrender is a decision. It is deciding not only to lay down your arms and stop fighting but a spiritual decision to lean into your wider sense of belonging in the world. This is what I did. I asked for someone to hold my hand. I got two. When you lean into the world, it somehow catches you.

Knowing when to surrender may be the most fundamental pillar of self-care. In the absence of control, you ask the Universe to take care of you, to provide exactly what you need. Even if you are unsure what you believe, surrender is recognizing you are not God. You are just one small human. Great relief can be found in moments of right-sizing our individual capabilities.

I challenge you to lean into the Universe. That is how you build faith. I challenge you to remember you are part of humanity. You are never alone. I challenge you to be vulnerable and ask someone to hold your hand when you are scared. I challenge you to look for the helpers every day. Notice who is helping.

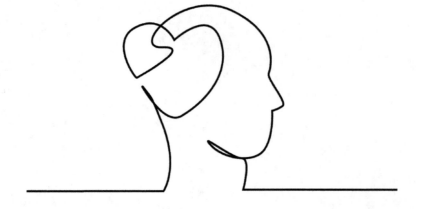

CHAPTER 4

TRUSTING YOUR INTUITION

"Instinct is the nose of the mind."

— Madame De Girardin

Has your body every known something before your conscious mind? Have you ever felt something in your bones that your heart, let alone your mind, was not yet ready to accept?

I first heard that still, quiet voice in the middle of the night some three months after the emergency C-section that saved Ian's life. The trauma left me with a deep, unreachable pain beneath my half-smile scar. My baby, still unsettled in his earthly existence, had been asleep for a rare stretch of some three hours. I was attuned to Ian's sporadic rhythms. When he slept, I slept. I rarely awoke when James, a medical resident, returned home. My body could not accommodate two people's unpredictable sleep patterns.

But for some reason, this time, as James crept back into the house, I awoke. It was as if, despite my exhausted body, my heart was awake already, waiting for him to come home. I lay there silently, watching him as he flicked on the dim closet light and removed his shoes and clothes, not making a sound.

Then, a scent reached my nose. It was not the smell of the hospital I'd become familiar with. This was the scent of cigarettes and something else utterly foreign. Was it perfume?

As James sat on the edge of the bed, preparing to join me, I sat up in the dark.

"What's that smell?" I asked.

"What?"

"That smell? It doesn't smell like the hospital."

"Jesus, Susan, what are you talking about?"

"It smells like smoke."

"Smoke?" He hadn't turned around to face me.

"Yes, cigarette smoke."

"Oh," he said, softening his tone. "There's a smoking lounge at the hospital. I had to walk through it to get to another ward."

"Wow, okay," I said. But something was rising from the ground up, and before I could put thoughts to it, the words popped out.

"It just occurred to me that you could have an affair," I said.

These words came up and out of me before I'd even had time to consider their validity. They bubbled up so simply and clearly that they shocked me, as if from a volcanic core I'd had no idea existed. This wasn't manipulation or passive aggression. It felt as though a belch had escaped before I could suppress it.

He did not turn around. I watched his back as he grew stone still.

"How could you actually think that?" he said evenly into the darkness.

"I'm sorry," I said, reaching out to touch his back, still baffled by my own words. "I don't think you're having an affair. I just realized it's the perfect setup. We have one car. You're always on call, so you always have a reason to come and go at odd hours," I prattled on, marveling at how easy it would be for him to cheat and amazed I had never thought of it until now.

He still didn't move or turn around.

I felt terrible that he thought I was accusing him. We fell asleep, his back still to me in the dark.

The next day, James called from the hospital, apparently still upset by my inadvertent accusation. I continued to backpedal, explaining the source of those words as much to myself as to James. But the genie was out of the bottle. No matter how much I tried to push the possibility back down, I couldn't.

This was in 1990. Though the term "gaslight" was born in 1938, from a play by the same name in which a husband slowly manipulates his wife into believing she's going insane, the term wouldn't become part of the modern lexicon for another two decades. In 2022, Merriam-Webster named it the word of the year.

This is the thing about gaslighting: We are more vulnerable to its effects when by trusting our own intuition, we threaten the image of life we so desperately want to hold on to. I was now in a full-on war with myself. My body knew something my heart was not ready to accept. My head played the role of propagandist. My husband only had to give me an explanation and, though my inquiring, logical mind still couldn't make sense of the stories he told me, I swallowed them whole, but they lodged in my throat.

Several months of incongruent stories passed. He looked hollowed out, a shell of the man who'd once loved me. I grew more anxious; my body continued to feel things my mind tried to stifle. By way of honesty, James finally told me he wasn't sure if he loved me anymore. I drew a hot bath, trying to catch my breath, hoping the warm water would stop my internal shaking. Seeing me in agony, he amended his comment. "Or, maybe I love you, but just don't want to be married to you anymore."

My bones ached. The heartbreak was deeper than the scar where my baby came into the world. I went to my parents in California, taking three-month-old Ian with me. James and I agreed he would use the time to figure out his feelings—he would tell me in three months what he wanted to do.

My parents did not view this as part of their role in any way. On the first day there, as I walked with my father, I told him I would try to get a part-time job to make a little money to pay for my stay.

"If you think we're going to watch your baby while you work, you have another thing coming," he said.

The sting of his words widened my feeling of isolation. I was alone in the desert with my husband. Now I was alone under my parents' roof. I slept in my brother's old room because my mother had quickly turned my childhood bedroom into her office. I spent my days reading to my wide-eyed baby and taking him on walks through the streets of a town that was no longer home.

Ian was my home, the two of us alone.

I called James every couple of days. But most of the time the phone rang and rang until I was greeted by my own voice from a happier time on the answering machine. I'd leave messages, trying to sound strong, but I was in purgatory, left holding baby Ian, who didn't sleep much, while waiting for my husband to love me again.

Finally, when I had been in Berkeley for almost exactly three months, James called.

I had my hair cut short in a current style. It showed my cheekbones and large eyes in a way I hadn't seen before. I stared at my image in the mirror, trying to decipher who I was, but all I yearned for was someone to love me. Loving myself was a concept that wouldn't come to me for years.

So, when James said into the receiver, "I think I love you," that was enough. "I'm ready for you to come home."

Growing up, I often heard my parents tell each other "I love you" as they talked about their day over a glass of wine with the kitchen door closed. They didn't use the L word with my brother and me. "You know we are very fond of you," my mother would say—and only when I was a little girl, crying into her dress. This is how I got a hug. She would add, "Are you just asking for attention?"

So even a lukewarm "I think I love you" from my estranged husband was enough to send me, if not back into his arms, back into his orbit. I immediately booked a flight and flew back to New Mexico. I arrived at midnight, carrying Ian, now six months old.

As I walked through the airport, a voice came over the loudspeakers. "Susan Gaines, please go to the white courtesy telephone for a call."

I picked up a white phone and James said, "Susan, we've been robbed. The police are here dusting for prints. I'll be there soon."

A half hour later, James was at the airport. He looked at me with a mixture of sadness and clinical observation. "You cut your hair," he said, cocking his head to one side. Then he added, "The police are still at the house."

When we arrived at the dimly lit house, an officer was indeed still there. Our eighty-five-pound Doberman exuberantly greeted me, but quickly went back to pacing, her nails clicking against the dark brick floors. I put Ian in his crib and sat staring numbly into the living room while James shuffled inexplicably through a utensil drawer.

I stared at the living room, at first not seeing anything. My eyes focused on a faint circle on the rug where the coffee table had been. It was a glass coffee table my in-laws had donated to our empty house. It was gone. I went into the kitchen to tell my husband and the officer, who was staring at the ceiling the way James had stared at my haircut.

"Why would you steal the blades off a ceiling fan?" The cop removed his hat and scratched his head. "Even for New Mexico, that's weird."

I could see the chalky shoeprint where a thief had stood on a chair and patiently unscrewed the blades. The officer surmised he'd found the tools he needed in our utility closet.

"They must have pulled up in a truck," the officer said. Then, turning to me, he asked suspiciously, "Where were you?"

"California," I said.

"A little girls' weekend?" he asked.

"Yes," I said, feeling as though my marriage was under scrutiny along with the burglary.

"Where was the dog?" I asked James, who still seemed to be looking for something in the utensil drawer.

"She was with me," he said, not turning around. Then he walked back into our bedroom, leaving me with the officer, whose badge glinted in the dimness: Padilla.

"Shit!" James yelled from the bedroom, which I'd been too afraid to see for reasons beyond the robbery. "He stole my shoes!"

I headed back there, the officer shadowing me. My dresser drawers had been flung open, my shirts and underwear strewn about. It was the second violation in which a stranger had touched my clothes. This time, my body wasn't in them, but the nearness of another man's body in my intimate space was chilling.

The TV was gone, leaving a dusty outline to remind us of what was missing. Strangely, the thief had left the computer and the stereo.

"They'll be back," the officer said ominously.

"For what?" I asked. "Socks?"

With that, the officer left. It was nearly 2 a.m.

James returned to the kitchen and absent-mindedly opened the refrigerator. "Oh, no," he said. "I forgot the milk. I'll go get it."

"It's okay," I said. "I can do without milk."

"I'll just go to the 7-Eleven and get it. I'll be right back."

Before I could stop him, James left, locking the door behind him. I shivered against the echo of the officer's words as I sat on the tightly made bed—it seemed like it hadn't been slept in for some time. Our dog jumped up and lay beside my tense body. We waited in the empty, violated house.

The convenience store was five minutes from our house. But after a half hour passed, James still wasn't home. It was nearly 3 a.m. I'd begun to shake from deep inside myself.

More than an hour after he left, my husband returned.

"Oh, my God!" I said frantically. "Where were you?"

His explanation was at the ready. "I saw the police had pulled over a big truck. The back was open, so I pulled over to ask if I could look to see if any of our stuff was in there. They said sure, so I looked, but none of our stuff was there," he said, distracted by something I couldn't see.

The story was implausible—and this time I knew it. But I had no other explanation, and it was nearing sunrise. As we fell asleep, our backs to each other, the bed smelled strange. It was as though my husband's very chemistry—the chemistry I had fallen in love with—had changed. A couple of hours later, I awoke to the unusual sound of silence. Ian was still asleep in his dark room on the west side of the house.

On the east side, where our bedroom was, inescapable light streamed in through the French doors. I turned toward it, wincing in the sharp illumination of all that was missing. Outside on the patio, James paced back and forth, his head down in thought, the dog in tow. Nothing made sense anymore. The light of New Mexico, once foreign and beautiful to us, now tormented him.

"Hell is no change," he'd say in reference to the never-changing cloudless blue sky that depressed him. When I dropped him off at the county hospital, I'd watch him disappear through the pneumatic doors that kept him cool, sealing out time and weather.

After the robbery, the only thing that seemed to energize James was when he thought he'd caught a glimpse of someone wearing his high-top Reeboks. He looked at every man's feet, yearning to confront the thief and take back the symbol of his carefree life before medicine.

But who would have known my husband and our Doberman were gone? And how? Was someone watching the house non-stop? Or was it someone who knew his schedule? Unscrewing the blades of the ceiling fan is not a quick job—and yields nothing usable or sellable. The robbery felt personal in a way I couldn't explain. Where had my husband been, with our dog, other than work?

In the days and weeks that followed, my body took on a life of its own. I was not consciously looking for anything. My hands would move before I knew why. Then the heat of guilt and shame would flood my body. Why, after seven years of marriage, was I suddenly questioning everything? Why didn't his absences make sense? I went through his belongings, his side of the closet, looking between folded clothes, scrutinizing our small credit card bills. I felt possessed by a power beyond myself.

It was as though my body's quest for reality overrode my mind's justifications for my husband's ill-fitting behavior. Each time my hands opened bills or went through his pockets, this force-beyond-my-understanding was rewarded with a new hint of a treasure hunt that I was now obsessed with. It turned out my soul craved truth beyond my immediate safety and comfort.

One day while James was gone for an entire weekend, presumably to moonlight in an outlying urgent care in a tiny New Mexican town, I slid my hand into the pocket of his jeans and withdrew a sharply folded piece of paper. My heart pounding, I unfolded it on the table where our TV had been, smoothing it flat over and over with my hand. There beneath my hand was a drawing of a young, shirtless, fit man. It was like a Disney caricature of James seen through the adoring eyes of the artist. The initials "M C" were artistically printed in the lower right corner.

The tiny town James said he was working in only had one hospital. I called and asked for him by name, telling them it was urgent. "We don't know anyone by that name," the operator said. "No one by that name is working here."

When James returned Sunday night, I showed him the drawing.

"Oh, that," he said flatly. "A nurse drew that."

"With your shirt off?" I asked.

He simply shrugged and said, "Look, Susan, I'm so tired. What's the big deal?"

A few days later, I found a credit card charge for a flower shop. It was dated the day I returned from California.

The great sages say intuition will always steer you to a better place. I was at war with mine. Its voice was an invader, trying to ruin my beautiful life. But the truth insists. My husband was now back at his regular job as a resident at the county hospital, so I paged him. When he returned my call, I asked him to explain the flowers.

"What was the date?" he asked.

"January 5," I answered simply. "The day I got back from California."

"Did I give you flowers?" he asked.

"No," I said. "I'd remember that."

"Weird," he said. "I'll have to figure that out."

"You think of a good lie and call me later," I said. There it was again, the words rising from some deep place of knowing before my mind could squelch, rearrange, or rationalize them away.

I had only one friend in Albuquerque, and I called her about the charge on the credit card, hoping she would help me rationalize it, which, at first, she did.

"Maybe they're for that friend of his whose mother just died," she said triumphantly.

"Yes!" I said, relieved, the possibility of my fairy tale life still intact.

I'd awaken in the middle of the night more than once to James talking quietly, reassuringly into the phone, while he sat on the kitchen floor using our landline. He'd told me it was his friend whose mother had just died.

"You could call the flower shop," my friend added. "It's your credit card too."

"I can't do that," I said. "It feels too weird."

"I can call if you want," my friend offered. "I'm sure it's for his friend. Come over with the baby, and I'll make you some tea."

As soon as I saw my friend's face at the door, my stomach dropped.

"The flowers were for a *Marisa Bella*," she said, before I even made it through the door. "Do you know that name?"

"M. B.," I said, as my stomach lurched. They were the artist's initials on the drawing of him I'd found folded neatly in his pocket.

"They even read me the note he sent with them. It was sort of cryptic."

So many things made sense all at once. My body had known. I wasn't crazy. By the time I got back home, James had left a message on the machine: "Hi. I remembered what those flowers were for. It was a nurse's birthday here, and I put the flowers on my card. I'm glad you reminded me so I can ask the others to pay me back."

I paged James repeatedly. When he finally called back, I demanded he come home immediately. He balked at first. But an unstoppable fire came up in me.

He came home, and I sat him down in a high-backed chair he'd found at a garage sale. I'd never liked it, and now it looked like an electric chair as he sat bolt upright while I paced in front of him.

"Who the fuck is M. B.?"

"She a confidante—"

"Whom you're having an affair with?"

"No, no. I just talk to her."

"Bullshit."

"She's a confidante—"

"Stop using that fucking word. You don't even speak French."

This went back and forth. Mother Truth would not let me rest.

"If you don't tell me the whole truth, I'll find her, and she'll tell me," I said, as he blanched. "She has nothing to lose. And you have everything."

It would take him another two days, but faced with my relentless questioning, he made a partial confession: He'd slept with her.

"How many times?" I asked, as if the right number would make it tolerable.

"Three," he said, as though he knew that was all I could bear.

I sent him packing. He said he would send her back to Las Vegas; he'd tell her once and for all it was over. He found a small efficiency apartment and moved into it. From that day forward, he tried to win me back. Mysteriously, I was never allowed to see the apartment, and though he wooed me with gifts and took me on dates, he did not spend the night. Even on Christmas, we opened gifts, but he left early to sleep in his own apartment.

Three more months passed. On New Year's Eve, James took me out in a dress he'd bought me that day. He got up from the table several times to use a payphone, saying he was calling work, though he was not on call.

After toasting the unknowns of the New Year, me looking into his eyes while he looked just over my shoulder, he drove me home.

As we walked up to the house at 1 a.m., the phone was ringing. James went to the neighbor's house to pick up Ian; I answered the phone. It was a woman asking to speak to James.

"May I ask who's calling?" I said in my most polite voice.

"It's Marisa," she said as though she'd called our house every day. "Was he out with *you*?"

"Yes," I said. "He is my husband after all. Marisa, Marisa—" All I wanted to do was keep her on the phone so I could finally get the truth.

"Bella," she said. "The Marisa he's in love with."

"Are you in Albuquerque?" was all I could ask. Just keep her on the phone.

"Yes. I've been living with him for almost a year. He's been lying to us both," she said.

"Thank you," I said. I gently returned the phone to its cradle as my husband walked in holding our sleeping baby.

I stopped him in the darkened entryway.

"You can leave," I said as I took the baby out of his arms. "Your girlfriend called. She's waiting for you back at your apartment."

"What?" he asked, incredulous. "What did she say? That must have been her friends. She wouldn't do that."

"Well, she did," I said. "And it's time for you to go. She's waiting for you."

I would love to tell you our relationship ended there. I certainly changed my focus. Bizarre, outlandish lies, unexplained disappearances, followed by deep apologies plagued my husband. I'd now have to base my sanity on my own inner compass. I knew I needed to get strong and get out of the house. I found a babysitter I trusted and took a job working lunch shifts at a nice restaurant.

I also started lifting weights at the university gym. I emulated good lifting techniques by watching others, mostly men, since few women were lifting in 1990. One of those I watched was a very handsome man with thick black hair. He was tall with a dazzling smile and kind, dark eyes. One day, that very same young man walked into the restaurant where I worked—he was the new valet and waiter.

Mateo and I began talking in the prep area like long-lost friends. Before long, I had told him everything about my husband's cheating, my new motherhood, and how all the rules of marriage had been broken.

James moved back in, promising that he was ready to make it work. I continued my flirty conversations with Mateo. Periodically, my husband would sneak out to make long-distance calls from a payphone or from our kitchen in the middle of the night. He continued to interview for fellowship positions in Minnesota, but up until a month before we were to move, he expressed doubts about me coming with him. I looked at depressing one-bedroom rentals in Albuquerque and tried to picture a life as a single mother.

"I could fall in love with you in a heartbeat," Mateo said one day.

My heart swelled with my first realization that maybe my husband was not the only love for me. Being loved—or nearly loved—helped me stand taller. Along with my growing muscular strength, through Mateo's eyes, I felt the charge of being beautiful without danger.

One weekend, when James went back to Minneapolis for a final interview, my childhood friend came to Albuquerque. She said, "Susan, I'll watch the baby. You go and do what you need to do. It's your turn."

Mateo and I went to see *Thelma and Louise*. He smiled at me in the dark as I sighed with longing and hope at the two women's reckless and brave pursuit of freedom. We drank champagne in a park—even getting a public drinking ticket to prove my rebelliousness. I saved that citation as proof there was life for me beyond my marriage. We snuck into little gardens in the university and talked all night under the New Mexican sky.

When James returned from Minneapolis, I picked him up from the airport. "I'm ready for you to come with me," he declared. "I'm sure."

"I met someone," I blurted out, still idling in the airport arrival area. "I'd like just a few days to figure out what you had more than a year to explore."

He was outraged. "You're just doing this to get back at me."

"You broke all the rules. They no longer apply," I said. For the first time I could remember, loving myself was more important than being "good."

"If you aren't sure you love me, don't come with me," he said.

"I'm not sure anymore," I replied. "I could stay here in the desert for a while, see if I could make a go of it by myself with the baby," I suggested, picturing Mateo being nearby.

After a couple of days, James shifted uncomfortably and made a plea that would ultimately keep our marriage together for many more years.

"You don't have to love me. But we have to leave the state the way we came in. Please drive out with me. All you have to do is put your body in the truck, and I will show you I love you for the rest of our lives."

As the spring winds picked up in Albuquerque, whipping sand into the house through invisible cracks, Mateo and I said goodbye.

"Go, make it work with the father of your baby," he said. "Never ever let anyone take you for granted again. You will always have a friend in New Mexico." We hugged with tears in our eyes.

I returned to our rented adobe, which had been so magical when we'd first arrived in the high desert three years before. James had packed the truck while watching Ian for the first time since his birth. I did as he requested: I put my body in the truck. We drove out of New Mexico with the couple of pieces of furniture that hadn't been stolen or sold. Our dog and baby were there with us in the cab. I silently watched the high desert give way to miles of open plains as we made our way to Minnesota, where I let him love me as long as I could.

I learned to love him, too, for as long as I could.

WHAT I LEARNED

"Gaslighting: The psychological manipulation of a person usually over an extended period of time that causes the victim to question the validity of their own thoughts, perception of reality, or memories and typically leads to confusion, loss of confidence and self-esteem, uncertainty of one's emotional or mental stability, and a dependency on the perpetrator."

— Merriam-Webster on the 2022 word of the year.

My husband's betrayal, then deceit, shattered me. But the worst part was not that he chose another woman over me and our marriage. It was how he manipulated my sense of reality. This behavior made me doubt myself in the most basic way. His betrayal insinuated itself in my mind and led me to betray myself. I couldn't trust what I knew. But worse than that, for months, years maybe, I was at war with my own deepest knowing.

James' deceit cracked the foundation of our marriage and ultimately led to its demise—but not until I fully accepted reality. That took another fifteen years. Though I now believe my then husband was faithful for the rest of our twenty-four-year marriage, I never completely trusted him again. I now know this distrust was because I never did the deep healing I needed to do. He never reassured me he'd changed. He only offered repentance. He apologized, but it was more out of fear of losing me than acceptance or even self-compassion about why he did what he did. We didn't heal; we just moved on. I lived in a strange in-between place, playing the role of loving wife without being able to fully absorb the love my husband was now bestowing on me. This is the steep cost of gaslighting: detachment from self and, therefore, detachment from intimacy itself.

SELF-CARE DISCOVERY EXERCISES

1. Recall a time when your intuition was trying to tell you something. Write about it.

   _____

   _____

   _____

   _____

   _____

   _____

   _____

2. Did you listen? How did you know it was intuition, not fear?

   _____

   _____

   _____

   _____

   _____

2. How does your intuition show itself? Is it an image? A voice? A knowing beyond your rational mind?

___

3. How can your intuition assist you going forward?

___

4. What is the relationship between intuition and self-care?

_____

_____

_____

_____

_____

_____

_____

TIPS FOR STRENGTHENING INTUITION

1. Notice when your intuition shows up.

2. Notice when you're trying to talk yourself out of a feeling.

3. Notice when someone else (who may stand to lose by you heeding your intuition) is trying to justify or explain away your feeling.

4. Remember intuition gets stronger as you practice and affirm its power.

5. Practice "reading" a room, sensing its energy. Do the same with people. Start with people you don't know.

SUMMARY

> "So often, when we feel lost, adrift in our own lives, our first instinct is to look out into the distance to find the nearest shore. But that shore, that solid ground, is within us. The anchor we are searching for is connection, and it is internal."
>
> — Brené Brown

Having turned a deaf ear to my intuition, only confirming it later with the trauma of my husband's unfaithfulness, I didn't know how to trust myself. Trusting our intuition and then acting on it may be the most courageous thing we can do. Intuition blasts through what we *wish* to what *is*. We are not always ready for what is. I was not. But in the end, the pain of maintaining a lie is far worse than the pain of seeing the truth.

Here's the thing about intuition: It will not let you rest until you attend to it. My intuition never gave up on me. It nudged me, poked and prodded me. It came to me in my dreams, brushed me in the breeze. It whispered, insisting I stop to listen. So, little by little, I began to trust the voice of my deep knowing.

When my mind finally made conscious what my body knew all along, I was relieved. But it would be many more years before I fully trusted my intuition was my most powerful sense. Eventually, my sixth sense became my superpower. I'm at the portal of this wizardry now.

Knowing when it *is* intuition is still a work in progress. Here are some of the ways my intuition shows itself:

1. It comes out of nowhere and makes no sense in the moment.

2. Sometimes, it comes in pictures or like a stuttering film. Only minutes or hours later, when the actual scene happens, do I recognize the premonition.

3. It bubbles out of me in words that come before I have a chance to analyze them. It's a knowing that insists on being brought into the light from someplace deep inside me beyond conscious thought.

Whether your intuition comes to you as the "Voice of God" or a quiet voice within, remember it is rarely convenient and sometimes impolite. Whatever you call it, you may not be ready to act on it, or you may even battle it. It often comes as a threat to the status quo. It takes courage to honor it. I challenge you to locate the voice or feeling of your intuition. I challenge you to heed its call. I challenge you to trust that even the hardest truths will help you live the life you are meant to live. I challenge you to shed the blanket of denial to see when you are being gaslit. I challenge you to stand in your own light and follow the voice of your higher self. I challenge you to find mentors, coaches, and friends who believe in your intuition and encourage you every day to lean into it.

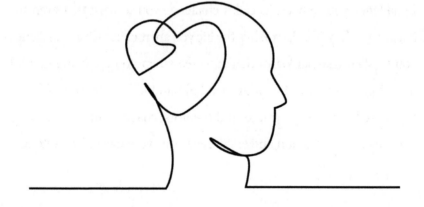

CHAPTER 5

TURNING JUDGMENT INTO COMPASSION

> "Mercy means that we no longer constantly judge everybody's large and tiny failures, foolish hearts, dubious convictions, and inevitable bad behavior."
>
> — Anne Lamott

Ian first brought the police into our lives when he was just two-and-a-half.

His exuberant, curious, stubborn nature made it hard for him to switch gears or "transition," as the parenting books on spirited children called it. The result would occasionally be a frenzied temper tantrum, during which he was utterly inconsolable and unreachable. When we first arrived in Minneapolis, it was springtime, a season on steroids in

Minnesota after six months of frigid temperatures, ice, and snow. For my part, I'd been delivered from several years of austere isolation, the experience of being abandoned, and then being reclaimed.

The giant elms arched over the street, creating leafy tunnels of dappled sunlight. Bright tulips, reflecting every color of the rainbow, danced in the gardens. My marriage, though still fragile, seemed to have made it. We moved into a beautiful flat, the upper floor of a duplex—just until we found a house to buy. I'd arrived in the land of abundance. Though I harbored a festering, deep wound from being cheated on, I was accepted by the South Minneapolis young moms, whom I assumed had never experienced the pain of betrayal. Their children also seemed to fall right in line. The other moms would speak in quiet tones and the children would miraculously listen. They were the parents for whom the books were written. You could "redirect" those children, use a "star chart" to reward them, and they would eagerly, joyfully go in the direction you wanted them to go.

That was not true with my son. One day before I left for some errands and a workout, I drove Ian and Carisa—the college student I'd hired not only to babysit, but to be a friend for me while my husband worked more than sixty hours a week—to our neighborhood coffee shop. Ian had his usual hot chocolate. Spilling was part of the routine, but the baristas replaced it at no charge. Later, some of the coffee shop employees would become his babysitters, too.

Before we got in the car, my verbal toddler wanted to count all the pumpkins on display outside. Then he wanted to count them again. And one more time. I finally got him to the car, where he insisted on getting into the car seat himself and then putting the seatbelt on. But then he scampered to the other side of the car, gleefully shrieking. He finally got into the car seat, but turned around backward so he could not be belted in. Maintaining my most even tone, I said: "I'm going to count to ten, and if you don't get in your seat and get your belt on, I will have to do it for you."

You may have experienced this sort of testing with your toddler. Suffice it to say, he did not turn around and put his seatbelt on. I wrestled him around and snapped his seatbelt around his little chest. I was sweating by the time I got behind the wheel. Carisa was in the passenger seat, her latte poised on her lap. Ian was screaming at the top of his lungs: "I want to do it myself!" He screamed this over and over until the phrase became a high-pitched shrieking that lost all meaning. I had read a lot about how to handle temper tantrums, so I did what the experts recommended: Once we returned home, I took off his seatbelt so he was not restrained, opened the car doors, and stood there with my babysitter/friend trying to remain calm, drinking our lattes. Eventually, he would burnout and fall asleep. He continued writhing and screaming.

Certainly, my back-fence neighbor did not hear Ian's words when she came to the fence and said, "What are you doing to that child?" I thought she was kidding. When I walked closer to the fence, I saw her expression was drained of any humor.

"Oh," I said. "You're serious."

"Yes, I'm serious," she said, from behind the fence. I could see her standing in the shadows of overgrown bushes wearing a faded floral housedress. "I am very concerned about that child."

"He's having a temper tantrum," I said, unable to think of anything beyond the obvious. The sting of judgment was so sharp I was rendered nearly mute. "You're welcome to come over here and see I'm not hurting him. That he's not being restrained. Haven't your kids ever had temper tantrums?" I asked, hoping to find common ground.

"Not like *that*," she said. "He needs help, and so do you."

She disappeared away from the fence, back into her house, leaving me more desperate than ever to calm my son. I peeked into the car and got close to his livid face.

"How about I give you a whole cup of chocolate chips?" I asked, resorting to a sugar bribe. But that only released him from the car. Like a swarm of bees contained in one small body, he flew out of the car, chased me, and tried to bite me. I picked up his little sweaty tense body and set him down inside the entryway, out of earshot. We sat at the top of the stairs until he fell asleep in a strange position as if sleep had waved her magic wand over him in the middle of his thrashing. I lifted him off the stairway, feeling his body finally surrender, his head heavy on my shoulder. His breath still stuttered involuntarily as the last of his sobbing left him. I gently carried him up to the apartment, flooded with relief and compassion for this child who could not regulate his emotions.

I sat down, careful not to rouse him. Carisa said something about the nightmare we thought was behind us when the doorbell rang. Carisa looked out the window to the street below.

"Oh, no, Susan. The police are here."

I stood and woodenly went downstairs, my child innocently sleeping on my shoulder. I opened the door to three beefy officers standing on the porch. I was keenly aware of what my neighbors might think should they witness this scene.

"We have a report that a child may be in danger here. Can we come in?"

"Sure," I said, waving them into the small foyer. "This is the child," I said.

"Your neighbor reports that he was screaming and that she's heard him screaming before," said the younger cop. "Want to tell us what happened?"

"Okay," I said, taking a breath. "Do you have kids?" When he said no, I thought this story would never make sense to him. I turned to the other older officer who was leaning against the mailboxes. "Do you?" I asked hopefully.

"Yes," he said, not smiling. "Five."

"Okay," I said, exhaling. "We were at the coffee shop. He wanted to count the pumpkins. Then again. And one more time. Then we got in the car and he wanted to put his seatbelt on, but he scampered around the car. I told him I would count to ten and do it for him if he didn't by then. I counted, but he didn't do it. I put his seatbelt on and he lost it. He has trouble with transitions," I said with a weak smile.

"All right," said the cop. "We just need to take a look at his little back to check for bruises."

All I could think of was, "What if there's a bruise? What if all his rough and tumble madness had left a bruise?" He was a wild child, who often fell off stools and couches and ran into things. Reflexively, I called Carisa to come downstairs. In some way I wanted her to witness, to help me bear up under this terrifying scrutiny. She descended the stairs, and as I lifted my son's shirt to the eyes of three officers, I broke down in sobs.

"Now, now," the older cop said. "Everything is fine. We're going to go back and tell your neighbor everything is fine. She was just trying to help. Wouldn't you have done the same?"

"No," I said. "I would have offered help. I don't even spank my child. Of all my neighbors, I am the only one who doesn't believe in corporal punishment. I would have offered empathy and actual help."

The officers shrugged. I watched their backs as they headed to their squad car and presumably to the neighbor's house to tell her all was well. The book was closed for them. But I was forever changed. I'd just been basking in the sense of belonging, the sense that I was one of this tribe of mothers. But now I'd been exiled by the opinion and phone call of a neighbor who didn't know me. I was forsaken.

For many weeks, maybe years, I was terrified to go out with my child because he might have a tantrum. I felt alone as a parent. I was married and financially supported, but utterly alone in parenting. Police, I learned, are the only people charged with the authority to physically take a child from your arms if they deem him or her in danger. They could have taken my child out of my arms and placed him on a seventy-two-hour-hold. This possibility haunted me.

I was a journalist at the time. I asked my editor if I could write a first-person account of my harrowing experience of being accused of abuse. "Yes," he said. "Write it." I went back and interviewed the officers who came to my duplex. I asked the younger cop how he had decided I was not hurting my child.

"You said you counted to ten. Abusers don't count to ten."

That, of course, is patently untrue. Abusers live in all zip codes and come from all cultural and racial backgrounds. They may also count to ten before they hit or hurt their child. His answer offered little insight into what had kept my child in my arms that day. This was a period when the pendulum was swinging from child abuse accusations falling through the cracks, leaving children to die at the hands of their abusers to false accusations of abuse leading to children being wrongly taken from their parents' custody.

I wrote the article, which was published locally. Letters of support poured into the editor. I dumped a pile of magazines on my neighbor's porch; she'd refused to answer my letters asking to meet with her. I continued to be horrified and ashamed that someone would think I abused my children or even spanked them. The article took on a life of its own. It was reprinted across the country in many local and national publications, including *Redbook*, nearly two years after the incident. The support was overwhelming and served to vindicate me. Almost.

I rejoined the tribe of Minneapolis moms—but never completely. I always suspected my son was different, his spiritedness greater than all the other children's. I had the sense of living just outside the community. Though I wore my disguise well for many years, looking like the other moms with kids who fell in line, I felt like an imposter now with two marks against me. For many years, like many spouses who've experienced an unfaithful spouse, I felt the cheating was because I wasn't as lovable as the other woman. Similarly, I believed like many parents, the proof of my competency as a mother was in how well behaved and conforming my children were. By this calculation, I was not only doing something terribly wrong, but I was fundamentally flawed. Not enough.

WHAT I LEARNED

> "Because true belonging only happens when we present our authentic, imperfect selves to the world, our sense of belonging can never be greater than our level of self-acceptance."
>
> — Brené Brown

The isolation and judgment I felt when my neighbor accused me of abusing my spirited son was the first of many lessons in letting go of the belief that we can control other people. I could not control my son—then or now—and I could not control what a neighbor believed about me. As a perfectionist and hyper-achiever—I was powerfully driven by what other people thought of me. My back-fence neighbor thinking I was a child abuser was one of my worst nightmares.

Being seen as a child-abuser, believing I was now outside of the "regular" mom tribe, made me identify with a group of women I'd never identified with before: child abusers. I began to wonder what it felt like to be a child abuser—not to hurt my children, but to be seen by the world as a monster. This led me down another rabbit hole: What if you were a parent who believed physical discipline was good parenting? What if I was from a culture that believed corporal punishment is the right way to raise a child? What if I weren't a white, middle-class woman, living in a middle-class neighborhood? What would that judgment feel like? What if I were a single, Black mother living in a working-class neighborhood and three white cops showed up? I began to strongly identify with women who were not my neighbors—women of color, single mothers, people whom the police do not always serve and protect.

As I began to identify with people, especially mothers, who might actually believe in corporal punishment or just haul off and hit their kids, a universal feeling of love began to grow in me. I began to feel that the "other" was me, just as I was seen as the other, a pariah. This new connection to "the other" made me feel less alone, more connected to the world. Any of us, after all, could be misjudged, or believe in different approaches to parenting. Few of us are actually monsters. Or, depending on who's judging, we're all potentially monsters.

We cannot control the actions or feelings of other humans. This territory was familiar to me. As the child of a mother with mental illness, I had the magical thinking that I could control my mother's behavior. To base your self-worth on a moving target outside yourself is a losing proposition. But it would be many more years as a puny human, trying to control my son's fierce will, before I finally surrendered to a power far greater than us both. From the moment he was born, Ian was my most powerful teacher on the spiritual journey I am still on.

Being the mostly single mother of a child who doesn't play by the rules taught me to dig down into the core of my life's purpose to ask: What really matters? What is this all about? My ego was deeply wounded by my neighbor's false accusation. But the call of motherhood was stronger.

Belief in my own goodness and worthiness was fortified by the shame and fear of what a stranger thought of me.

I have been paired with my children in this life for reasons I am still delighted to discover. Parenting them has always been about letting go as courageously as I hold on. Their paths were etched out in their earthly lives long before they even arrived. I am lucky enough to be their earthly guide—and they mine.

SELF-CARE DISCOVERY EXERCISES

1. Recall a time when you were unfairly judged. What did it feel like? What was your response, outwardly and inwardly?

_____

_____

_____

_____

_____

_____

_____

_____

2. When, past or present, have you based your self-worth on how other people are behaving? What beliefs are behind this association of self-worth with other people?

_____
_____
_____
_____
_____
_____

3. How has the experience of feeling judged—rightly or wrongly—affected your compassion for others you might otherwise be quick to judge?

_____
_____
_____
_____
_____
_____

4. How does judgment, either yours or someone else's, serve to strengthen your sense of loneliness and isolation, perfectionism, and imposter syndrome?

　
　
　
　
　
　

5. Recall times when you felt deep compassion for someone who did not look or seem like you. What happened? What lasting effects did this compassion have on you?

TIPS FOR TURNING PAIN INTO SELF-CARE

1. Compassion and curiosity are the antidotes to judgment: When you feel yourself judging or another judging you, turn on your curiosity and compassion.

2. The road to belonging runs through compassion: When you can put yourself in another's shoes, you are suddenly part of a much larger tribe.

3. The salve for perfectionism is vulnerability: When you're working so hard to appear and be perfect, ask yourself what you're afraid of.

4. Disconnect your worthiness from the false idea that you are better than others.

SUMMARY

> "Your children are not your children.
> They are the sons and daughters of Life's longing for itself.
> They come through you but not from you.
> And though they are with you, yet they belong not to you."
>
> — Kahlil Gibran

Our worthiness, our right to be at the table, to belong to our community, cannot be based on how our children, parents, or partners behave. Each of us has our own path to walk. Other humans are not our projects. Our children are not an extension of ourselves. If we make them so, we are doomed to feel a chasm of unworthiness. Over time, I learned I was no more a bad mother because my son was struggling than I was a good mother because my daughter was doing well. I am grateful for both parenting experiences, which taught me both my children are expressions of "Life's longing for itself."

"In your longing for your giant self lies your goodness," wrote Kahlil Gibran.

You, too, are good, not because of the good behavior of those around you, but because you are here to do big things. You are here to find your path. Self-care is the practice of honoring that path.

I challenge you to explore your beliefs about your worthiness. I challenge you to loosen your grip on the importance of any of your roles—whether at work or home. I challenge you to feel the longing for your giant self. I challenge you to ask yourself who you are beyond "mom," "dad," "daughter," "son," "lawyer," "doctor," or "laborer." Whatever your perceived identity, you are so much more. I challenge you to tap into the essence of who you are, to let go of perfectionism, to join the human tribe. You belong. You are not alone. I challenge you to allow imperfection as an invitation to others to also be themselves. I challenge you to feel your belonging through vulnerability.

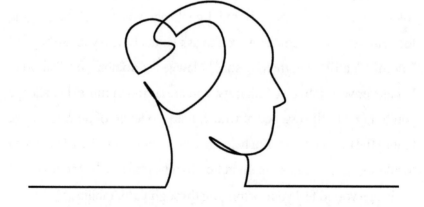

CHAPTER 6

LOSING YOURSELF

"Secrecy lives in the same rooms as loneliness."

— Abraham Verghese

Have you ever found yourself having no idea who you are? You finally stop running and you can't figure out even the smallest thing you want or need? Have you ever become so enmeshed with your identity it becomes a stand-in for who you truly are?

Somewhere on the long drive out of New Mexico to the more civilized Minnesota, James and I made a tacit agreement: *He owed me.* He would owe me for the rest of my life. I would put my body in the truck. In exchange, he would try to make up for what I believed he'd stolen.

James did what he promised: He loved me in every way he could. He showed his love by letting me choose the house, the decorations, the way we remodeled it, and with loads of cash, which he liked to count into my hand with each paycheck. In exchange, he was rarely home, working at the hospital more than sixty hours a week. He went to bed long after I did, claiming it was the only time he had to himself. He awoke at 5:30 a.m. to hit the gym and start all over again. When he was home, he was so exhausted he'd sometimes close his eyes and nod off at the table.

I would get the external life I'd been holding out for: a beautiful house in Minneapolis on a quaint residential street near the creek. But I would raise the kids mostly alone, with James playing the supporting role with phone calls squeezed in between patients, for whom he was always running late.

I began to believe the role I was playing: the sacrificing doctor's wife, the full-time mom who kept a lovely home. We went on to have another child, a beautiful daughter, Kate. We looked like we had it all and, in many ways, we did. But there was a chasm between appearances and my deep, unhealed wound. In this deep divide, I was alone. I computed James was loving me, but it was as though I was cocooned in glass. I could not receive it. While my husband was complying with the actions of love, I was unable to absorb it or ever feel I deserved love—from him or anyone.

Meanwhile, I was keeping secrets. The biggest of all was that I would never trust my husband again. And worse, I no longer respected him, as I had my father, a man I thought beyond reproach. I tried to hide my loss of trust and respect from everyone, especially our children. I wanted more than anything for them to believe in their dad, to believe in our love. Nestled in that secret was the seed of my loneliness.

Loneliness is born of secrets. My secret was this: While I was trying so hard to be a perfect wife and mother, I felt unworthy of unconditional love. I was unable to truly receive love, to feel its warmth. I didn't let anyone get close to me because I was terrified that others would learn my life was not as it appeared. My friendships were only for appearances, too. For a deep person like me, superficial relationships are exhausting. And lonely.

While I felt unworthy of unconditional love, I did believe I deserved the fruits of my husband's hard work: money. He continued to put piles of cash in my hands. I used the money to hire more help: a cleaning lady, more babysitters. I was so lonesome sometimes that I felt as though I was about to crack into a million little pieces, each one yearning for connection. So, I took the money my husband gave me in exchange for his presence and bought myself presents. Clothes—expensive clothes.

I had one boutique I frequented. Sometimes, it seemed as though my car drove itself to the store. I bargained with myself. "I'll just see if there's a parking place in front," I'd say.

If there was easy parking, I'd say, "I'll just see if there's a sale." But I wouldn't make it to the sale rack. Once inside the store, the shop ladies shouted with joy, "Hi, Susan!"

It was like having friends. Almost. They were more like drug dealers, feeding my addiction. My hands would sweat as I signed the credit card receipt. I would leave with thousands of dollars' worth of designer clothing, giddy and full of shame. I'd hide the clothes in the closet for a few days, like hiding liquor bottles.

The more I spent, the less justified I felt in asking James to spend more time with me and the kids. The feeling of abandonment deepened. Loneliness became anger. I began to relish spending his hard-earned money. Don't forget: He *owed* me.

Resentment, entitlement, loneliness, shame, anger—round and round we went, until my shopping addiction was inextricably linked to his workaholism. *But he owed me.* I'd become a well-dressed, unhappy woman in my late thirties. And under my beautiful clothes, my body had begun to hurt. I'd developed a pain behind my shoulder blade. It had become so tight I could not take a full inhale. It was an episodic thing I'd chocked up to Tae Kwon Do and generally being a hard-working person. I had to work to deserve my pay. I was tirelessly driving my kids to lessons, games, playdates, camps, and anything to make their lives perfect. I saw muscle pain as a token of my hard work. Usually,

I'd just push through with annoyance. I saw pain as an inconvenience, certainly not a messenger.

One day, as I sat in the quiet, empty living room, I asked myself a question in the non-judgmental, caring tone I reserved for my children: "What's going on?" I was greeted with silence. So, I sat with myself. I sat with my pain. I asked again: "What's happening, Susan?"

No direct answer came. But something in my kind attention unwound the pain just a bit. Gradually, I could hear the thin, weak voice inside me, like a forgotten prisoner: *I am so lonely. I am tired. I have no idea what makes me happy. Who am I?*

Not long after I confronted the stranger living inside me, I began to make friends. One night, I was out with James having a drink together. It was one of the rare ways we "connected," though it was often with him staring straight over the bar and me with my full body turned toward him. A few seats away, two female friends were having a drink together—something I had never done. They began talking to me.

"What do you do for your arms?" one of them asked. I was wearing a sleeveless shirt, and apparently my rigorous workouts showed. I was so excited to talk to them, as if I'd been locked away for years. I eagerly told them I did chin-ups and they could, too. I found out later they'd been trying to guess the nature of my relationship with James. Were we friends? On a first date? Married? All were, in a way, true.

We bought them a drink and they bought us dessert. We exchanged numbers, and soon they introduced me to other women in their circle. For the first time since junior high, I had a group of female friends— real friends who loved me unconditionally, though I could not see why.

As these friendships all but filled the hole of loneliness, I weaned myself of my addiction to shopping. I had enough clothes to last many years, anyway. Little by little, I began to share what had happened in my marriage. They listened compassionately, not judgmentally, never asking me why I was still married to James. They opened a pathway of possibility. They modeled what it could look like to live as independent, single, smart women on modest budgets of their own making. They would also eventually serve as heart-centered entrepreneurial role models; they showed me what it could look like to serve others in a healing role and make money doing it.

WHAT I LEARNED

> "As long as you keep secrets and suppress information, you are fundamentally at war with yourself."
>
> — Bessel Van Der Kolk

Unhealed trauma had locked me inside myself. Without a therapist, coach, or close friends, I kept my pain hidden from even myself. Though I tried to connect with James, it ended up mostly being a rehashing of my anger at his betrayal. He would tolerate my anger—because *he owed me*—but I never got what my soul was looking for: a discerning, courageous look at why he'd done what he'd done. All the apologies in the world didn't add up to self-awareness. That is what I craved from him. I wanted something real, beyond the dissatisfying simplistic explanations. More than anything, I wanted to believe in him again, to see him as ethical, trustworthy, and brave. But I couldn't get that back.

I built my new life in Minnesota on a cracked foundation. I got my husband's love, or at least commitment, but it did not penetrate my isolation. It was not enough. That left me feeling guilty by turns, wondering what was wrong with me. I finally had the perfect life, but it wasn't enough.

My disappointment and hunger for connection created a hole I tried to fill by buying beautiful clothes. From the outside, I looked like I had it all. I can even see now I was pretty—and adorned with understated, Italian-made clothes. But in the few photographs from that time in my thirties, my smile was dim. I feel for the isolated young woman I was, trying to do it all, while silently yearning for social and intimate connection.

I had a rigorous checklist of what it meant to "take care of myself." Proper sleep, healthy food. I worked out regularly. I became a third-degree black belt in Tae Kwon Do. I even started writing a novel about my time in New Mexico called *Another Man's Shoes*. But I was alone. I did not allow anyone to see my sadness and disappointment—and consequently, I felt no one really knew me.

All the activities and talents in the world cannot make up for lack of friendship. Being admired is not the same as being loved. Achievement can make you feel good for a moment, but you're always looking for more—especially if you base your self-worth on it. The quest to be "the best" is exhausting. I finally found friends—or they found me. Little by little, I made myself vulnerable. I also eventually found a therapist. So began my years of self-discovery and healing. But it would still be several more years before my soul's voice was loud and strong enough.

SELF-CARE DISCOVERY EXERCISES

1. Write about a time when you lost yourself to a role or a lifestyle.

_____

_____

_____

_____

_____

_____

2. How did you know you had lost yourself? What were the signs?

3. How do you talk to yourself when you're hurting?

4. Do you have real friendships? What's your definition of friendship?

5. How does true friendship support self-care?

TIPS FOR NOT LOSING YOURSELF

1. Create a "body map" showing where you feel different emotions in your body.

2. Ask yourself, "What's going on?"

3. Let pain or discomfort be your messenger.

4. HALT before you shop or ingest food, drink, or drugs, and ask yourself, "Am I doing this because I am *hungry, angry, lonely,* or *tired*?"

5. Get yourself a community of supportive friends you can be totally honest with.

SUMMARY

> "There is more wisdom in your body than in your deepest philosophy."
>
> — Friedrich Nietzsche

I'd become lost in a false identity, lonely in my secrets. Gradually, my body led me out and helped me find myself. First, I had to listen. I had to sit with the feeling of not knowing what I needed or who I was. Self-care is about listening and asking yourself questions. That's what I began to do. At first, I was met with silence. But in the end, the questions are more important than the answers. Asking questions about what you need and want are *acts of care*. They are the beginning of telling yourself you matter.

By asking and listening for the answers, my own unique brand of self-care began to emerge. I began saying *yes* to things I needed and *no* to things that got in the way. Self-care isn't about checking off a to-do list created by self-care influencers. Only *you* know what's good for you. Self-care is the caring attention you give to your own needs at any given moment. It isn't about navel-gazing. It's about learning to monitor your own energy, spirit, emotion, and physicality to be in sync with the world around you.

I was torn from myself because of my secrets. But my body wasn't fooled. I was tired—the sort of tired a full night's rest doesn't cure. I had chronic muscle pain—right behind my heart. "That's the back of your heart," a physical therapist once told me. "That's where you store all the things you aren't ready to deal with yet. It's your emotional backpack."

As I began to unpack that load with a therapist and friends, my pain went away. I began to love myself. Though it remains an ongoing struggle to pull back from the drive to achieve, I am learning just to be me; most of the time, I now know I am enough. I challenge you to discover what self-care means to *you*. I challenge you to know when you need a friend. If you don't have a true friend, go out and find one. I challenge you to be your own best friend, to talk kindly to yourself and ask yourself questions about what you need. I challenge you to listen to your body, learn its language, and honor it. I challenge you to be with yourself, your hunger, and your pain—to not run from it, but to stay.

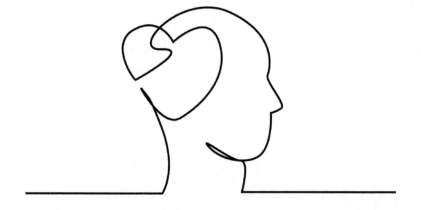

CHAPTER 7

BECOMING A WARRIOR OF THE HEART

"Every act of creation is first an act of destruction."

— Pablo Picasso

With my eighty-five-pound Doberman and my black belt, I was well-protected. I lived in an idyllic neighborhood near a meandering creak hugged by walking paths. This natural swath was home to owls, deer, and every few years, a bobcat. Minneapolis city planners had struck a rare balance between natural habitat and city life—especially in the upper middle-class neighborhoods where we now lived.

For the first time ever, I could walk at night—not down by the creek where I feared predators of the supernatural kind. But on the rare nights James was home with the children sleeping, I was able to walk for several minutes at a time without surges of flashback terror and lose myself to awe and gratitude: This was my life. We lived here. In a beautiful 1929 Tudor. *My lonely, lean life in New Mexico had somehow paid off*, I'd think, as I marveled at the cozy lives inside the softly lit, genteel homes. I imagined how inside those homes, the inhabitants felt safe and loved. Yet, deep down, I felt my husband's unfaithfulness had made us imposters in this world. We didn't really belong in this neighborhood of love. I imagined no unfaithfulness had marred the lives I glimpsed from the darkness of my nighttime walks.

Even living in the land of predictability, tradition, and outward niceties, I wasn't safe from the monster within. Even my body and posture reflected this self-doubt. I was outwardly fit. I lifted weights and continued to practice martial arts three times a week. By many accounts, I'd achieved the female physique the media touted. But my shoulders rolled forward. I hunched, protectively hiding my heart and the womanly chest outside of it.

Trainer after trainer would comment on this rolled-in posture, offering to "fix" it with various exercises. This response only added to my feelings of being outwardly judged and even sculpted by men. Even with all my muscle and training, my body was still not mine. Martial arts and weight training had taken me far. I'd built a fortress. But the story of heartbreak and sexual assault was inside my fortress, not outside. No matter how well-dressed, fit, and well-groomed I was, nothing could protect me from my own beliefs and the terror of being revealed as less than perfect. This was not really my party. I was not worthy of being here.

Even getting into the master's program at Northwestern University's Medill School of Journalism came only after a fight. For my bachelor's degree, I'd gone to University of California Santa Cruz, a fine school, harder to get into than UCLA. But they didn't have grades. Though I'd graduated with honors, without an actual grade point average, Northwestern, a traditional private college, rejected me outright. Then, after meeting with a dean and almost throwing up with fear, he sent me out with orders to get some real-world experience writing for local publications. I built my portfolio, volunteering with local papers, while working a full-time cubicle job in downtown Chicago for $10,000 a year.

While working my Chicago cubicle job, I signed up for night classes and was able to procure glowing letters of recommendation. The next time I applied to the master's program, I was wait-listed. This was a step closer. I met with professors on the admissions committee, where it became clear the problem was with my state school background. But finally, after dogged inquiries, I finally gained admission. Once there, I excelled, graduating with top honors. Still, the fact that I'd had to work so hard to be admitted made me question my right to be there. Even with my master's degree, I felt like an imposter. Sometimes, I still catch myself in the belief that if I don't work harder than everyone else, I don't deserve to have a seat at the table.

Soon after moving to Minneapolis, I was invited to the brainstorming editorial meetings of a startup city magazine, and after throwing out a few ideas about fitness, they decided I should be the health and wellness columnist. I wrote my first column about boxing—me, then a not-quite forty-year-old mother of two, writing about boxing. I wrote it in the first person. After that, my editors asked me to write all my pieces in the first person. I was being paid to explore all sorts of athletic endeavors. Soon, for the first time in my life, I saw myself not only as a martial artist, but as an athlete, a mover.

When I tried the graceful, rhythmic, healing exercises of the Gyrotonic Expansion System, I quickly realized I was experiencing one of the most intelligent movement systems around. This was different. After just one session, I knew it could be life changing. I took three private sessions so I could write about it, but I was hooked. For the first time in nearly twenty years, I felt my chest opening, and my shoulders began to naturally slide down and back. My hands came down. My fists opened. Change began to happen inside me, too. I softened. I became more vulnerable. I began to see the world through a more open-hearted lens. There is power in vulnerability. I was no longer hiding. When you aren't hiding, you have less to fear.

My vulnerability poured onto the page. My column became more personal—for example, how bike riding made me feel free and safe because I believed no one could catch me. This was another way to write about how assault had left me feeling unsafe when I walked.

The readers, especially Minnesota readers who tend to avoid sharing anything personal, loved this. They felt seen and heard. My editors renamed the column "Personal Gaines," which was like a Minnesota version of *Sex in the City*. Here I wrote about my life, not only my fitness life, but beyond.

My column connected to people far beyond my neighborhood. Sometimes, I caught people staring at me in a restaurant and realized they might recognize me from the photos accompanying my monthly column.

My friendships also benefitted from my vulnerability. I began to trust that I was lovable not for my perfection but for my mistakes, my struggles, and my positive belief that we can all persevere and triumph over hardship.

This was the land of Minnesota Nice, a place where it was hard to get to know people, but their sense of tradition, the cultural value of predictability, and the way they look out for their neighbors in the deep, silent snow continues to be a lifeline for me. For a woman who grew up in the land of political upheaval and earthquakes in Northern California, this stability gave me a foundation from which to grow my wings.

As my body, especially my heart, began to open, I craved movement to perpetuate this opening. When I went to martial arts practice, my hands went up, and I minimized the area an opponent could strike. This physical stance also perpetuated my mental relationship with the world. I kept myself protected and somehow smaller so there was less to hurt. It became clear it was time to leave my twenty-four-year practice of self-defense. What had for many years provided me with self-confidence and safety was now keeping me small. If you keep defending yourself, you will always find something to defend against.

Predictably, the master instructor, a white man from Minnesota, tried to shame me into staying at the studio. I had, after all, created a following of women and men who recognized my depth of understanding and ability to convey the techniques of the best practitioners of form and sparring. I'd started my own classes, sparring for women only, and a white-belt class attended by mostly black belts looking to refine their technique.

"You don't know everything," the master said, wagging his finger at me over his desk.

"I know I don't, sir. But I need to go out into the world and learn more about who I am."

I shook his hand and bowed. He would no longer control my life, while I would forever embody the tenets of Tae Kwon Do, which we shouted in unison before every class: courtesy, integrity, perseverance, self-control, and indomitable spirit. The dojo is a place where even a male-dominated sport like Tae Kwon Do transcends gender in recognition of finesse, speed, and power in any body. I had quite literally earned my stripes. Walking away from it demanded I know who I was beyond my stripes and my third-degree black belt.

Though my relationship with the school and the master had become unhealthy, based on guilt and obligation, it was a family of sorts—my family. Now I was leaving it. Even my children, though now moved on to other sports, had acquired their black belts from the school. We were a black belt family. No matter how badly I felt inside, every time I went to class, I was reminded with bows and "Yes, ma'ams!" that I was respected and admired.

I had been married to Tae Kwon Do. It had supported me, protected me, and given me a sense of self-worth. But it had taken me as far as I could go. I was afraid and excited as I left the studio behind me, walking into the cold January air under a leaden sky. Though I did not yet know what I was looking for, I'd just created the space for something even deeper. It was the space of trusting the world as a potential friend rather than a foe, when you put down your arms and let your heart sing.

A few months later, I asked James for a separation. It turned out leaving Tae Kwon Do, where I'd first met my husband twenty-four years before, was a practice run for leaving my actual marriage. Though we'd built a strong working relationship over the fifteen years that had followed his affair, I was growing at an exponential rate from the inside out.

Through mindfulness-based meditation, therapy, Al-Anon, yoga, and the Gyrotonic method, I was expanding, evolving, and finally becoming happy.

Somewhere along the way, I had stopped waiting for my husband to come home. While James continued to work himself to the bone, providing us with all the material riches we could dream of, we were not together. If I was going to continue growing, we had to separate. It was no longer possible for my wings to remain clipped. Though I had no idea what I was flying toward, I knew I must get all impediments out of the way if my heart was finally going to take off and soar. I came to discover that home was a place inside myself.

WHAT I LEARNED

> "In the process of letting go, you will lose many things from the past, but you will find yourself."
>
> — Deepak Chopra

Stepping out of the familiar into the unknown *by choice* goes against every survival molecule in our bodies. Perhaps the scariest part is that we are choosing it. I could have easily stayed in my marriage. I was not abused. I was well taken care of. Only a generation before me, women did not have such a choice. To willingly cast ourselves out of the home, away from the familiar, into the cold feels spoiled at best and downright reckless at worst. It is also not a choice for women of lower-income households. While it is true my financial situation was by all measures secure, it was nonetheless terrifying to willingly leave the known for a situation that easily could have—and turned out to be—worse than the one I had. Every fiber in my body asked, "Why would you cast yourself into the cold for an alternative you don't yet know?"

Perhaps this is the same question so many ask themselves when climbing Mount Everest. There is a longing for expression, freedom. In a relationship, individuals can only grow so much. If one person remains steadfastly fixed, the other will be tethered as well. Separating and ultimately divorcing remains an experience of loss for me. Losing that relationship was the experience of my first death. Yet in initiating the separation, I was not causing the death, but rather heeding my soul's yearning that had been launched years before when my husband first broke our vows in the desert.

The truth is you can't learn what's next until you first create space for the unknown.

The fastest way to change is through the body. By learning to trust your body, you can also begin to trust your mind, heart, and spirit. Be at home in your body. If you are not, find a way to make friends with it.

SELF-CARE DISCOVERY EXERCISES

1. What does home mean to you?

   _____
   _____
   _____
   _____
   _____
   _____
   _____

2. Recall a time when you chose to leave the familiar without knowing exactly what was next. Looking back, what did it open up for you?

   _____
   _____
   _____
   _____
   _____
   _____
   _____

3. What do you secretly wonder if you really deserve?

4. What positive things have you learned through your body? What are you reinforcing with your body?

5. When have you compared your insides to someone else's outward appearances—for example, the way I looked into other people's homes from the darkness of my walks?

___

___

___

___

___

___

___

TIPS FOR BECOMING A WARRIOR OF THE HEART

1. Practice vulnerability to free yourself of imposter syndrome and give others courage.

2. Move in heart-opening ways to practice the physicality of vulnerability.

3. Notice where you're clinging to familiarity—even if it's unhealthy or no longer serving you.

4. Practice abundance. Happiness is your birthright. You are worthy of love, but it must start with self-love.

SUMMARY

> "Home life ceases to be free and beautiful as soon as it is founded on borrowing and debt."
>
> — Henrik Ibsen

You can't live off the energy of emotional debt forever. The body is the most accelerated path to mental and spiritual transformation. As I moved from self-defense to heart openers, my deepest beliefs began to change. By aligning myself differently to the world, my expectations and experience of it also began to change.

One day, I noticed my shoulders had naturally moved down and back. This change wasn't a forced military posture or a parent telling you to stand up straight. It was my body knowing it was safe to shine my heart. When I did, I was rewarded with the feeling of being seen, of no longer hiding. It seemed the world had been there waiting to love me all this time. It had been waiting for me to shine my light, to walk with confidence—waiting for me to come home.

If my body could move with such grace and openness, what else was possible? What stories have you been telling yourself that have limited your view of the world and your potential? I challenge you to recognize the difference between the safe familiar and the challenge of the new. I challenge you to walk into new worlds, even if it's just taking a new path to work. I challenge you to live in abundance, to believe there is more than enough for everyone. I challenge you to believe happiness is your birthright. I challenge you to take that first step into the unknown. I challenge you to make your body your home so you will never be homeless.

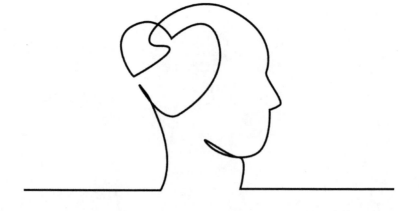

CHAPTER 8

LISTENING FOR YOUR ANGELS

"God, grant me the serenity to accept the things I cannot change, the courage to change the things I can, and the wisdom to know the difference."

— Reinhold Niebuhr

My son Ian was on a path to hell. It seemed to have nothing to do with the privileged, educated life he was born into. He was pulled toward this path from the moment the neighbor called the police—or earlier—when he was born by emergency C-section. He tore open my worldview and tried to show me from his birth ten days early that I could not plan another human's journey. He did nothing according to plan. He was unsettled in his being, squirming in discomfort, both tiny and wide-eyed. He was at once too small and too old for a comfortable existence on earth. He learned to talk in full sentences by the time he was fourteen months. His first words were not "Momma" and "Daddy" but "sky" and "bird." From the beginning, my son's focus was beyond his earthly life. He was already on a journey far beyond the comforts of home.

By the time Ian was three, around the time the neighbor had called the police, he was telling me about his past lives. "Remember a long, long time ago, when I was a teenager?" he asked me once as we pulled into a parking lot. I tried to reorder the sentence for him, but he roundly corrected me. "No, Mom. A long, long time ago when I was a teenager." Years later, when he was a teenager, I so wished I'd asked him what he had already known when he was born, what he was finishing or reenacting in this life as a teenager. But that may not have mattered any more.

Ian was first arrested at thirteen, almost immediately after starting public school as a young ninth grader. He'd been skipped to third grade, halfway through second grade, as the school's solution for his precocious, intelligent nature.

The days preceding his arrest were also an intense experience of my own psychic power. This was the second time I'd had a premonition. The first was concerning my husband's affair in New Mexico. Ian was obsessed with a new friend, the sound of whose name caused the hair on the back of my neck to bristle. It was the "y" at the end of "Bill," or so I told myself, that caused this reaction. But really, I had no explanation for what I knew: My son's fascination with this boy was going to bring him a load of trouble. I faced Ian in his bedroom, looking at him directly.

"I know you're in trouble," I said. "But it's not too late."

Ian looked at me, visibly shaken. "Mom, you look like you're looking right through me."

"I'm not looking through you. I'm looking into you," I said. Then from the depth of my being came these words: "I can see you're in trouble. It's not too late to get out, to change course. But Dad and I can't help you if you're in jail."

"What?" he said. "Oh my God, Mom, what?" I thought the same thing: *What?*

Three days later, Ian, the son of a doctor and a stay-at-home mom with a master's degree, was arrested for firing a high-caliber bb gun into the back windshield of a moving car—after Billy told him to do so.

The high-school police were frisking my son daily. I learned this not from the principal but from Ian. I approached the school administration, asking to partner with them, to help me parent this child whose father was a medical doctor working more than sixty hours a week. I took Ian to therapists, who diagnosed him with Oppositional Defiant Disorder, ADHD, and other nebulous terms that got us no closer to helping him navigate the world.

I'd become as vigilant as a deer, sensing where and when the world posed a danger to Ian. But despite my hyper-alertness and sometimes psychic sense of what was about to happen, I was unable to save him from bad things happening. Perhaps nothing is worse than having psychic visions of bad things happening to your children and being absolutely unable to change the course of events. I was a deer, but in a corral.

Three is a magic number. Or at least I had to hear the same thing three times before I heeded the directive. The first time, a friend in California said it. I was telling her about the latest escapades with Ian. I spoke in a high-pressured, breathless way, like waves crashing one into the other. "Have you ever heard of Al-Anon?" she asked. She proceeded to tell me how it was the sister organization to Alcoholics Anonymous. "It might help you."

I'm not the one who needs help, I thought, silently outraged. Hadn't I presented myself as the perfectly rational, thoughtful mother, giving everything to save Ian's life? My friend's suggestion only served to make me work harder to save his life—and present the story in a way that invited only admiration. The second time I heard the suggestion was on an airplane, from a total stranger, no less. In my calmest, most rational way, I began telling my seatmate about my son and the challenge of being his mother.

"Have you ever heard of Al-Anon?" she asked.

This time, I could say I had. I listened patiently as she told me how and why it might help.

"Help me fix my son?" I asked.

"No," she said. "Help you live with the unfixable."

Unfixable? I only had to try harder, care more. Then, I could pull Ian out of the trenches.

The third time came from a home computer repair man. He was working on my desktop and checking internet connections in my tiny dormer office when I picked up the phone to make a call. Ian was on the extension downstairs.

"Oh, sorry," I said. "No. I wasn't trying to listen to your call."

That's all the computer man heard. And maybe a sigh when I hung up the receiver.

"Is he having trouble?" he asked.

"No," I said. "I guess I don't know exactly what you mean—"

"If you think he might be doing drugs, he is," said the computer man-turned-oracle.

"I mean, maybe some pot or something, but—" I sputtered.

"There are a lot of things you can do that will make the situation worse," he said. "There's one thing you can do that will make it better."

My curiosity overtook my shock at his courage. "What's that?"

"Go to Al-Anon," he said.

It still took me a few months, but one day, as I sat fretting about whether Ian was at school and whether I'd receive another call about his misbehavior, I decided to find an Al-Anon meeting. What was the harm? The first meeting I found was for parents of children with drug and alcohol issues. When it was my turn to speak, I announced that I was probably in the wrong place, that my son really didn't have a problem. The other parents nodded, smiling with familiarity at my denial—which annoyed me. Their easy-going understanding made me want to shake them. How did *they* know?

Later in the meeting, a man said, "My daughter just got out of treatment. I'm so angry with how she behaved. I just put that anger on a shelf while she was getting help. Now that she's back and doing okay, I'm trying to figure out how to take that box down and start to unpack it."

I started to cry. Something about having to put emotions on a shelf and save them for later undid me. There was the little emotional backpack again. When I left, someone said, "Come back again." I did. I went back to Al-Anon almost weekly for eight years.

Within two years, Ian was expelled from the entire school district. Despite daily frisking, the police could find no evidence for what they believed to be drug dealing. They finally illegally confiscated his phone, watched text messages of kids looking for drugs come in, and used this evidence to permanently expel him. He was fifteen. I was a psychic mom with plenty of financial resources, but essentially a single parent. I threw every resource I could find at Ian, while my daughter Kate made her own order out of chaos, carved her own path to success, and patiently waited for me to see her in all her glory.

A local Catholic school, known for being a second-chance institution, admitted Ian to eleventh grade. When he made the varsity soccer team, it looked like it might be the turning point. But he soon missed practice, saying he couldn't find his shoes. He wreaked of marijuana. We got him into his first treatment program for youth at Hazelton. Twenty-eight days and a family program later, he was released back into our care. He not only went back to his ways, but he escalated his drug use, feeling compelled to continue a journey that had been apparently laid out before he was born. He soon said he just couldn't go back to high school. He was sixteen. He took the GED and passed, saying he would go to community college. But the drug use and criminal activity only escalated.

We hired a professional interventionist who confronted Ian as he emerged groggily from his bedroom one morning. For nearly two hours, we told him how his lifestyle was affecting us. The interventionist, who told us he himself had become sober at age fifty, sat in the corner of our living room like some sort of dark angel, grounding me—if no one else—in the steady belief that I was standing up for Ian, against the demon of addiction. The intervention created an opportunity to witness the struggle with Ian's body and spirit for control of his higher self. In the end, he chose to walk out into the cold, taking what he could carry with him, unwilling to go to the treatment center we'd found for him in Montana. For now, addiction had won.

Despite our daughter Kate's crushing sadness, I hired a locksmith who changed all the locks. I began to pray. Growing up in a non-religious household, it seemed silly at first to get down on my knees and ask God to look after Ian. But Al-Anon had taught me the only chance for my first-born child was to let go, to turn him over to God. All I knew was nothing I'd been doing was dissuading Ian from the path he was hell-bent on travelling. So, I prayed. I prayed and prayed and prayed. *Please God, keep him safe. Please God let him hear your voice.*

I found a small photo of Ian when he was five years old. The complex depth of his hazel, flecked eyes was far beyond the years of his little body. I stared at that picture, feeling my heart so full of love for the boy born too early by emergency C-section. I focused on the pure spirit of the child born to me, not the man-child who swore at me and who'd inserted himself into an underworld that was swallowing him whole.

Ian became homeless at sixteen, bouncing from one danger to the next. Occasionally, I would buy him lunch, steadily offering him a way out. Meditation, prayer, and yoga began to ground me so finally that during one such lunch, I did not cry as he told me about his deep sadness at seeing a drug dealer with a two-year-old child. "You know you can go to treatment any time," I said. "There's a bed waiting for you."

"I know," he said, tears streaming down his face as his food sat untouched.

"Do you feel like you don't have a choice?" I asked.

"I know I have a choice, Mom," he said. "But for some reason I keep choosing this."

I hugged him goodbye, hoping it would not be the last time I'd see him alive.

After a few months, Ian finally agreed to go to the wilderness-based treatment program in Montana. Even that was not smooth going. He threatened to run away multiple times. Then when it finally looked as though he'd make it through, three days before Christmas, I got a call from the director that Ian had punched another kid in the face. They had a zero-tolerance policy, and I had to get him out of there. Now. I pulled over to the side of the road and sobbed. The staff gave me phone numbers for a boot camp and an escort service to ferry him from Montana to Idaho. If he cooperated with the bootcamp, he could return to finish treatment.

I hired two men I didn't know to "escort" my son to Idaho in the middle of the winter just before Christmas. Ian called me from the escort's cell phone, telling me how awful and cruel I was—but now I knew he was safe. He faxed us letters from bootcamp, telling us they'd taken his shoes so he couldn't run away from the teepees they'd set up in the snow. "They even tell us when to spit while we're brushing our teeth," he wrote. "If we want to turn left, we have to turn right and then all the way around." He drew a diagram for clarification. I smiled, trying to picture my son doing anything someone told him to do. When Kate smiled at the same spot in the letter, I knew he was okay.

Ian made it through bootcamp, returned to treatment, summitted a peak, and finished sober and proud. Meanwhile, I'd finally decided to insist on a separation from James. Through various family weeks we'd attended and my growing awareness through Al-Anon, it became apparent to me Ian was not the only one with an addiction problem. James was a high-functioning drug and alcohol user too.

That Valentine's Day, James and I lay in bed together crying because we had to try living apart.

We took money from Ian's college fund and sent him to an aftercare program in Seattle. He did not make it through the first month. A friend bought him a plane ticket, and $10,000 later, one month's installment, he'd abandoned his group as they left an AA meeting. It was Valentine's Day. He slept at the airport for two days, waiting for his flight. He called me from the airport to let me know he was okay.

"You know how I know I'm okay?" he asked me.

"No," I said, still exhaling my relief that he was, for now, safe. "How?"

"Because I've been sleeping right next to the airport police office," he said. "I'd never do that if I was using! You know what's weird, though? This lady cop thinks I'm homeless. I asked her why she thought that. She said, 'Well, you've been sleeping here for two days, and you don't have any luggage, only the clothes on your back.' Well, that's true, I guess, but homeless? Oh, and Mom, I'm also reading a really good book." He sounded like the kid he was before high school—curious, enthusiastic, and alive.

"What book are you reading?" I asked.

"I saw it before I left the center. I liked it because it fit in my back pocket.

So, I took it," he said. "It's called *Man's Search for Meaning* by Viktor Frankel. It's amazing," he added.

Man's Search for Meaning is a powerful memoir about surviving a Nazi concentration camp. The author explores the search for purpose and meaning in life, even in the direst circumstances. And it happened to be the same book I was reading—yet another testament to the psychic connection I have to my son.

Though he may not have known it, Ian's return home stalled the separation between his dad and me. For a few days, we all tried to return to our family roles and relationships. But it was like trying to glue a pot that had broken into tiny pieces. It never looked the same again. Within a few days, Ian was using again. I kicked him out and resumed the process of separating from James. I found myself at the table with my fourteen-year-old daughter. It was so quiet without the drama of her brother—just the two of us, quietly eating at the table. Kate told me a story about her day, and I laughed.

"You're funny," I said.

"I know," she said, matter-of-factly. "My friends think so too."

That's when I realized I didn't know Kate at all. It was her turn to be known. It was her turn to be seen. And what a delight it was to see her.

James moved into an apartment downtown that he said was haunted. Dark energy came to visit him on three occasions, chilling him to the bone. I privately wondered if it was payback for breaking my heart and eventually our family. Ian moved in with a friend in a house full of guns, drugs, and a huge, unneutered pit bull. The house was raided by the police more than once, but nothing stuck. A night in jail was not going to "scare him straight." He was nineteen, with two treatments under his belt and at least two arrests. I kept praying.

The night before Kate's high school graduation party, Ian was up all night in his father's parking garage, hallucinating, trying to take videos of "people who were spying" on him. I was concerned he might be having a psychological break, showing signs of schizophrenia. At the graduation party, full of neighbors and friends, Ian moved around like a nervous ghost. He was terribly thin, his eyes circled in darkness.

"Is that your brother?" one of Kate's friends asked. "He's so small."

The young man who'd inspired awe in his sister's male friends was now a boy again—a diminutive wreck of himself. Several times during the party, he sidled up next to me: "Mom, look. *Look* at this video of the people who were watching me last night." When James and I finally agreed to watch it, we couldn't see any of the people Ian said were hiding behind pillars in the garage.

One day in the early spring when the days were growing longer, but the trees were still bare, I picked Ian up for lunch. He wore a fraught expression and a fresh scar along his jawline.

"What happened to your face?" I asked.

"That's not the worst of it, Mom." He twisted himself in the passenger seat and lifted his shirt to show me a puncture wound. "Someone stabbed me."

I tried to get the story out of him, but I quickly realized I would not get the truth. The details weren't important. Something bigger and darker had descended. I could feel it fill the car. Whoever, whatever this force was, it was trying to kill him. I went home, called my parents, and asked them to give him shelter in California—in the house I'd brought him to when he was a baby. The baby they'd refused to take care of when he was four months old was coming back to them again. This time, they did not hesitate.

"Send him," my mother said.

The night before he left, Ian's friend came over wearing a bulletproof vest. He stayed until I drove Ian to the airport in the early hours of the morning. I prayed and prayed some more.

Ian joined AA for youth in Oakland, California. He was on fire. "It's like a gang of sober people," he said with excitement. They were indeed former gangsters, ex-cons, and criminals who'd managed to claw their way out of the darkness into the light of sobriety. They were the only type of people my impressionable son would listen to at that point. Ian did what they said, walking miles and miles, memorizing the *Big Book*, and attending every sober event he could find.

This lasted a few months, until a friend Ian had met in AA died of a heroin overdose in the alley of the Tenderloin district of San Francisco. He was twenty-one.

I learned later that while some of the most intense gangsters stayed sober, the white, upper-class kids broke off into a gang of their own, switching from oxycodone to heroin, moving from snorting to smoking to injecting it. They'd become their own gang of junkies.

WHAT I LEARNED

> "When we are no longer able to change a situation,
> we are challenged to change ourselves."
>
> — Viktor E. Frankl

Al-Anon continued to save me from a powerful societal expectation, expressed in an offhand comment I once heard at a congenial neighborhood barbeque: "You know," the neighbor said, "you can only be as happy as your least happy child." Implicit in her statement was the idea that not only is it difficult to be happy when your child is struggling, but if you are not as miserable as they are, you are a bad parent. I battled this adage every day.

"If I was only as happy as my least happy child, I'd be in a fetal position under a table somewhere," I told her, my anger rising.

Al-Anon and the phrase we read aloud at the beginning of every meeting was the antidote: "We, too, were lonely and frustrated, but in Al-Anon we discover that no situation is really hopeless and that it is possible for us to find contentment, and even happiness, whether the alcoholic is still drinking or not."

I left the barbeque that day and headed directly to an Al-Anon meeting, where I was learning bit by bit I would be of better service to everyone if I learned to be happy, even when my son was not. By working the Twelve Steps myself, I found hope. I was beginning to accept I was powerless over Ian's addiction, and I began to embrace the "Three Cs" of Al-Anon:

I did not cause it.

I cannot control it.

I cannot cure it.

I was learning to change the only thing I could: me. This change of focus from my son, whom I had no power to change, to myself was restoring me to sanity. My focus on bettering myself was like working out myself, rather than begging someone else to go to the gym. I had to learn to be happy, even if my firstborn was heading down a road of destruction. While actual happiness was still a long way off, I was beginning to embrace the idea that I had a duty to parent *both* of my children. I needed to parent my daughter too. It was Kate's turn.

SELF-CARE DISCOVERY EXERCISES

1. What have you been trying to change that is not in your power to change?

   _____
   _____
   _____
   _____
   _____
   _____
   _____
   _____

2. Have you been doing the same thing over and over while expecting different results?

_____
_____
_____
_____
_____
_____

3. Where do you need to exercise courage to change the things you can? Name some of those things.

_____
_____
_____
_____
_____
_____
_____

4. How have your angels been trying to get your attention?

5. Where do you struggle to know the difference between what you can and cannot change?

TIPS FOR LISTENING FOR YOUR ANGELS

1. Look for animals. (I notice cardinals when I'm on the brink of transformation, for example. Deer show up when I'm struggling.)

2. Listen for different people saying the same thing to you. Heed their words.

3. Notice when you're trying to change other people. That's their work. What's yours?

4. Turn on all your senses. Get quiet.

SUMMARY

> "It doesn't matter who says it, as long as it gets said."
>
> — Anonymous

I saw the above quote high up on a telephone pole while I was waiting at a red light. What made me look up? Way, way up? I had to strain my neck to look that high up on the pole, but there it was on a piece of wood nailed to the pole. It was reinforcement for listening to wise words, regardless of who says them. I'd received the same message from three different people: Go to Al-Anon. At first, I tried to shake off the power of the suggestion by discounting who the speaker was. Who is this guy, anyway? A stranger in my home, fixing my computer. But the power of his words seemed prophetic. His courage to speak to his customer in this personal way made him more of an oracle than an IT contractor. You never know from whence wisdom will come. You never know what form your angels will take.

Angels are everywhere. If we listen deeply for their voices, we can spot them. Look for their appearances—it might be in numbers. Three is my number. Three people told me to go to Al-Anon. It was time to listen. Nothing I'd been doing was working, so I had nothing to lose doing something different. I let go of my end of the rope—no more tug of war. I let go of the illusion that if I just tried harder, I could turn my son's journey in a new direction. This was perhaps the hardest direction change I would ever make. Just as I'd surrendered in childbirth, I surrendered in parenting. That is perhaps Ian's most important lesson for me: surrender.

I challenge you to look at what you are holding tightly to. I challenge you to loosen your grip. You are just one tiny human. Great relief is to be found in accepting your humanness. Even if you don't believe in God, I challenge you to stop trying to be one. If you do believe in God, try turning it over to that power. Faith is a muscle, a verb. You strengthen it by practicing it.

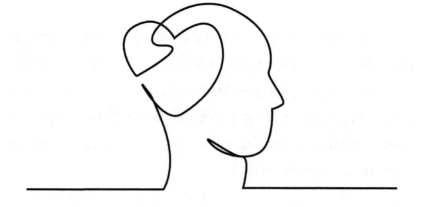

CHAPTER 9

RELINQUISHING YOUR POWER

"As I began to love myself, I found that anguish and emotional suffering were only warning signs that I was living against my own truth."

— Charlie Chaplin

It was May in Rome. I was there for an international Gyrotonic conference and three-day certification. I'd begun practicing this fluid, healing exercise system for a health and fitness column I wrote, and I'd fallen in love with it during my research. Its gentle, non-judgmental approach allowed me to truly begin to listen to my body, peel off the layers of defense I'd built through martial arts, and finally begin to stand in my own power. It was changing me from a well-defended martial artist to a more fluid, sensual, feminine being. The practice was releasing my inner mermaid; though I wouldn't know it for years, the practice was healing my sexual trauma, allowing me to reclaim my naturally fluid, sensual, and easy way of moving in a space where it was physically and psychologically safe.

The certification group was made up of mostly Italian ballet dancers, women who rolled their eyes and spoke about the American woman at least fifteen years older than they were in Italian. There was a sprinkling of gay men. And Marcos who, by the way he found me in the lunchroom every day, led me to believe he was heterosexual, despite the tight little black T-shirts he wore, which in the US might mean "gay." In Europe, I figured it was something else. Either way, his dress showed off his well-sculpted muscles—belonging not to a dancer, but a weightlifter.

Marcos was Spanish, though he had lived in Belgium his entire life. He spoke four languages—all with a cute accent. After our rigorous physical certification, he moved out of the female friend's flat he'd been staying in and into mine. He said she kept trying to make the relationship more and he was over it. I felt like the chosen woman among all those beautiful Italian dancers.

Marcos' skin glowed like polished oak as he stretched out like a Greek god on the mattress we'd pulled onto the floor of my flat. The sex was transformative, altering. I was drunk with oxytocin. Under his touch, I was a queen. At forty-five, and under his gaze, his hands, I was ageless, pure beauty without self-consciousness. I was a liquid dancer, a poet, a maestro of sensuality. He was the picture of physical perfection. His body was his full-time job. And it showed.

"Why haven't you ever been married?" I asked.

"I was waiting for you," he said. Marcos had just enough gray hair to convince me he was mature and meant what he said.

By the end of the week, he took my face in his hands and told me he loved me. My knees went weak with the sensation of a fairy tale becoming real.

That was it. I was alive. I was on fire.

The etymological connection between "Rome" and "romance" more deeply sanctified my belief that we were meant for each other. Never allowed to believe in Santa Claus, because my mother didn't want to "lie" to me, the idea that perfect love could show up transported me, overtook me. True love did exist! Santa was real! There truly was such a thing as getting everything you wanted!

The fairy tale spun out before me as a story only waiting to be discovered. The butterflies that overtook my body every time I saw Marcos that week were only further proof we were meant for each other—not that sexual attraction is a drug our bodies produce to make us blind. The idea that we'd been out there for each other all this time—and that this was our time—took my breath away. It also drove me to protect it at all costs.

When I was back home, we talked daily on Skype. I'd set up my laptop on my bed. Marcos sat in a dim room because it was nighttime in Brussels. I'd learn later the light was dim not by intention, but because he only had a few lamps. His internet connection wasn't the best either. His face would often fall apart in a Picasso-like stuttering image and then freeze. I'd wait as patiently as I could, trying to recall the actual image of the man who'd said he loved me as we'd walked through the cobblestone streets of Rome, hip to hip, arm in arm. Now, his mouth on his forehead like a third eye, I'd stare at the decomposed picture of a man I really didn't know.

Three months after the beginning of the fevered dream, I flew to Brussels. We were to drive from there to the Alps where we'd stay in a *gîte*—a rustic mountain bed and breakfast—and hike the mountains as he'd done annually for a decade.

Marcos met me at the airport. His skin was less the color of oak now and more like espresso, as though he'd been lying in a tanning bed—which it turned out he had. His apartment was dusty and dark. Brussels was cold, the buildings set back from the street, hidden by hedges. He kept cash in a can under the sink rather than a bank so he wouldn't have to pay taxes on his income. The stove was more like a camping stove with the gas turn-on underneath. And he had women's hair products in the bathroom. When I asked him about them, he said he had no idea they were for women and berated me for being possessive. I was hooked. Nothing, but nothing, would interrupt the fairy tale I was clinging to with all my might.

Marcos had a beautiful blue Saab, which helped negate the nagging feeling he was penniless. I later found out it was a marker on an unsettled debt of $10,000 Euros from a wealthy client for whom he did "in-home" personal training. The fact that she was Swedish royalty only served to feed the fairy tale. In his beautiful car, he drove me ten hours through two-lane roads in the French Alps. Without guard rails, cliffs dropped just feet from the passenger side where I sat. When a car came the other way, Marcos had to back up, sometimes a quarter of a mile, until there was a little space on the inside of the road to pull into. The entire trip was an exercise in faith.

No one spoke English, but everyone tried to communicate with me. I'd taken four years of high school French and thought I'd finally have a chance to practice speaking and listening, but Marcos had little patience for that. Occasionally someone would offer to speak English, but he'd tell them to speak French. I became invisible. I'd sit for hours as the French language swirled around like white water rushing down from spring ice melt, numbing my brain, and leaving me in a sort of loneliness even deeper than in my first marriage.

But that didn't stop my fairy tale. The *gîte* was clean and simple, with wood-planked floors. An open floor-to-ceiling window framed the Alps and trails, which we hiked every day. Marcos would often leave me behind on the trail since he viewed each hiking day as a personal training session. I was in solid physical shape, but the trails were steep switchbacks that left me breathing hard and glistening with sweat. Multigenerational families passed me in the other direction using walking sticks. "*Bonjour!*" they'd sing more than say. Their joy and belonging served to make me feel even more alone.

One day, Marcos was at least twenty minutes ahead of me on the trail when I began to feel a familiar burning in my urethra. A vague spasm hinted at a urinary tract infection. At first, it came and went, convincing me all was well. But by the time I caught up to Marcos, the burning was steady and increasing. It was a Sunday in a tiny village in the Alps. We stopped for a beer, and in French, he asked a waitress if she might know what to do for a urinary tract infection. It turned out she was an expert in herbal remedies; she recommended what American girls have also always used to self-treat urinary tract infections: cranberry juice.

As I squirmed in my seat, the pulsing pain increasing, I told Marcos the infection was beyond cranberry cures. I was going to need an antibiotic and a painkiller. He drove me down the mountain into a bigger town. By the time we arrived, I was moaning in pain, terrified I'd be unable to endure the pain. The only way out would be driving off a cliff. We found an open pharmacy on a Sunday: the first miracle. He spoke to the pharmacist in French, telling him cranberries might be the answer. "*Non,*" the elderly man said with flat certainty, looking at me writhing in pain.

Angels are everywhere. This one was in the French Alps in a pharmacy on a Sunday. This angel proceeded to dispense a horse pill of an antibiotic and an anti-spasm medication he said targeted the urethra. I downed the pills. I didn't care if it was poison at this point. Anything to put me out of my misery.

But the pain got worse before it got better. I cried in agony as Marcos drove me back to the *gîte*. He left me alone in the room as I writhed in pain, saying there was nothing he could do for me so he might as well go downstairs. Another hour would pass before the medicine began to work its magic.

I'd been so overcome with pain that I missed this first sign of Marcos' lack of empathy. I was so relieved to be free of pain that everyone around me seemed miraculous, most of all Marcos. By day, the fairy tale held up, as my brain methodically, quickly discarded anything that would contradict it. But our dreams will show us the truth we cannot let into our conscious minds.

The night I'd overcome the urinary tract infection, I had a prophetic nightmare I thought was about my son. It may have also been about Marcos, who'd become my drug of choice. The morphine-like effect of being with him had temporarily numbed my growing concern for Ian, who continued to descend into addiction and the crimes associated with the all-consuming nature of the illness.

In the dream, I was in a tiny village tucked back into steep mountains, almost like a cave. Everything was in shadow. Muscular man-baby cherubs, like those in Rafael's famous 1514 painting *The Triumph of Galatea*, were all around. Somehow, Ian was transmuted in the dream into a grotesque, terrifying convergence of infancy and manhood. I awoke sweating, heart pounding, and filled with foreboding—which I projected onto my son. Only now do I also see my subconscious was screaming warnings about my relationship with Marcos.

I ignored them all. Only separated from my first husband for a year, I believed no one would love me like Marcos. The only way to keep the relationship going, I believed, was to get him to the United States. The "easiest" way to do that was through marriage. There was no proposal, just a momentous tumbling toward what felt like the inevitable. The way to make Marcos mine was to marry him. Only in retrospect did I see his decision to marry me was more like calculated acquiescence; worst-case, the marriage would end after four years (the amount of time the Immigration and Naturalization Service needs to deem a marriage legitimate and remove the conditions enabling the foreigner to gain permanent residency). If he could make it for four years, Marcos would have a road to citizenship, which was his secret dream. I knew this because he'd tried and failed before with another woman. Why didn't I see that as a red flag?

Though the case stalled out more than once, with the help of an immigration lawyer I hired, Marcos and I were married. Within another year and a half—which qualified him for his conditionally-based green card—Marcos walked into a fully equipped fitness studio I'd secured with a home equity loan, a personal training client base I'd already created, insurance, a bank account, a car we purchased soon after his arrival—and me.

Marcos' kind, humble mask came off almost the moment he arrived in the US as my husband. He was cold, aloof, and secretive. He didn't speak to me for days on end, only occasionally punctuating the silence with a mean comment. At first, I chalked these cold moments up to cultural differences, language barriers, or adjusting to a new life in the US.

After a few days of withdrawal, he'd set a bouquet of grocery-store flowers, still wrapped in plastic, on the counter with an apology. His weapon of abuse was withdrawal, emotional coldness, and gaslighting. If I asked what was going on, or insisted he come back to the fold, he would accuse me of being possessive, demanding, or needy.

As the reasons for marrying him quickly dried up, I reasoned, if it was only about the sex, so be it. People have married based on worse reasons, I thought. But very soon, the sex disappeared as well. He would parade around the bedroom naked, slip into bed, and say the timing wasn't right or he wasn't in the mood. For the first time in my life, I began to feel compassion for all the men expected to initiate sex, only to be rejected with, "I have a headache."

Kate went off to college, grateful to be leaving the stink of microwaved broccoli—Marcos' soulless, flavorless way of eating vegetables—and his body odor which emanated from his tight-fitting polyester black T-shirts. After months of the silent treatment from my daughter (which I'd chalked up to teenage angst), Kate told me how she was sure Marcos couldn't wait for her to leave the house because of the way he treated her and her friends. I reprimanded him and told him in no uncertain terms, "This is her house. You need to treat her and her friends accordingly." After that, he was more cordial—until she left.

Marcos became practiced at using his weapon of choice: emotional and physical withdrawal. To live with him was to experience the trauma of abandonment repeatedly and then be told, "It's all in your head." Meanwhile, our studio was growing. I drew clients from social interactions, mostly with women, while he also attracted female clients, many of whom he solicited at coffee shops or the gym. A few times a month, a new woman would walk into the studio to see Marcos. He would not introduce us. For all I knew, they simply thought I was another teacher at the studio—rather than his wife and founder of the studio.

After a particularly long bout of being ignored, I would ask him to leave. But Marcos would only buy flowers and say he wanted to work it out. I dragged him to couples therapy, and for two sessions, he maintained an honorable façade. I tried to believe he was still invested. Later, I realize he was acutely aware of the four-year time conditions on his green card. He still had another year.

WHAT I LEARNED

> "The most common way people give up their power is by thinking they don't have any."
>
> — Alice Walker

Sometimes we may be so starved for love and affection that even breadcrumbs can seem like enough. Denial is so strong it can mask the strongest insights, the most prophetic dreams, our body is trying to tell us. I'd not only married a man, I'd married a fairy tale that I fought fiercely to protect as long as I could. Despite growing evidence to the contrary, my fairy tale was about "true love" and "second chances." To let go of the marriage, I believed, was to let go of my belief in these ideals. I was not ready to do that.

Practicing the Gyrotonic method had helped me connect to a sensual, feminine side of myself I'd been robbed of through sexual assault. Through the experience of self-defense by way of martial arts, I'd first become confident in a masculine way. Now Gyrotonic was helping me experience femininity in a whole new way. But it made me vulnerable to a new kind of hurt.

As I vehemently embraced my restored sense of sensuality and beauty, I was at first unable to see the reality of how this shark had captured me. It was my fierce grip on the story—not Marcos—that took away my power and perspective in the relationship. I wanted so badly to make everything fit that I abandoned myself by tolerating meager rations of love and affection. Until I loosened my hold on the story of "true love" and "second chances," I would not be able to end this, once and for all.

SELF-CARE DISCOVERY EXERCISES

1. When have you badly wanted to believe in a story you'd told yourself about a relationship or a job?

_____

_____

_____

_____

_____

_____

_____

_____

_____

_____

_____

2. When were you in denial? How did your body try to break through?

_____

_____

_____

_____

_____

_____

_____

_____

_____

3. How have you abandoned yourself?

_____

_____

_____

_____

_____

_____

_____

_____

_____

4. Have you ever allowed yourself to be mistreated? What did you learn?

___

5. What are you tolerating now?

___

6. Where, when, and to whom do you relinquish power?

_____
_____
_____
_____
_____
_____
_____
_____

TIPS FOR RECLAIMING YOUR POWER

1. Check in with yourself. How are you feeling?

2. What are you trying to talk yourself into or out of?

3. What story are you telling yourself by accepting less than you should?

4. Who were you being when you allowed yourself to accept breadcrumbs? Who are you being now when you can ask for the whole loaf?

SUMMARY

> "To me, this is the ultimate power: to be comfortable with ourselves and to be our own soulmates. Soulmate means one who remembers, who knows, and who can master themselves by taking care of their own feelings, thoughts, and body."
>
> — Sister Dang Nghiem (aka Sister D)

When I tolerated and excused Marcos' withholding of affection and companionship to preserve a story, I gave up my power. I believed a strong physical relationship meant he was my soulmate. I also believed love like that would never come again. This story appealed to me because I fundamentally believed I wasn't enough, wasn't lovable, and wasn't beautiful. So, when he episodically abandoned me, it served to further prove a deep-seated belief instilled in me from the beginning.

When I look back on that time, I am flooded with compassion for myself—and for all the other men and women who do this to themselves: Allow others to dictate their fundamental lovability and beauty. I gave away my power by believing another human held the key to my innate lovability.

When we don't love ourselves, how can we expect others to love us? No single person's love can fill the hole left by lack of love for ourselves.

That hole is bottomless. First and foremost, I abandoned myself when I stayed in a relationship fed by breadcrumbs.

I challenge you to notice where you abandon yourself. I challenge you to learn what it means to be your own soulmate. I challenge you to look in the mirror every day and say, "I love you. You're beautiful." I challenge you to admit what you are tolerating. I challenge you to fearlessly look at all of yourself. When you no longer hide anything from yourself, you are free.

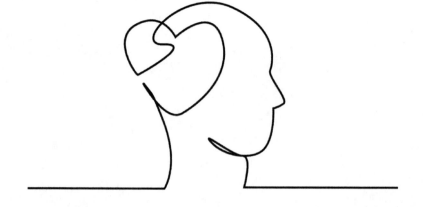

CHAPTER 10

FINDING FREEDOM

"Rock bottom became the solid foundation on which I rebuilt my life."

— J. K. Rowling

When I first learned Ian was in jail, I cheered. It was five days after I'd seen him, wild-eyed, head shaved, emaciated. He was twenty-three. We'd just had a cup of coffee at Starbucks where he'd been contrite about his latest brush with the police. But just five minutes later, he was sitting in my car on the passenger side, no longer sorry. He talked feverishly, telling me the police were wrong, and he was not only going to get all the contraband back, but he was going to get money from the government for having wronged him. I'd looked around the busy grocery store parking lot, reassuring myself I was not alone. I couldn't wait to get him out of my car. I was also poignantly aware it might be the last time I saw him. I feared for my safety and, just as strongly, I feared for his. *By the end of the week*, I thought, *he will either be in jail or dead.*

For so long I'd thought, *This can't be happening. He's the son of a doctor.* As though being a physician's son would somehow give us a pass on addiction and the dangerous road Ian had chosen; that somehow, with all our access to treatment (he'd gone to several treatment programs), therapy, good schools, and anything else money could buy, our son would be spared. Though to this day, Ian attests to a peaceful, loving upbringing, being the son of a doctor did not inoculate him against the dark addiction that seduced him.

When Ian's phone went straight to voicemail five days after our tense meeting, I prayed he was in jail. I did a Google search on his name and birthdate, holding my breath. *Please, please, please don't be in the morgue.* When his name came up connected to a county jail, I pumped my fist in the air, danced around the room, and shouted, "Yes!"

For now, death had passed him by again. I prayed they'd keep him this time, one last chance to save his life—and possibly the lives of others, too. Ian was moved to the workhouse at its maximum level of security. Like prisons, workhouses are secured facilities with guards, cells, and solitary confinement. But they are geared toward people serving shorter sentences, being offered more programming, and having the opportunity to leave the facility to attend work. There'd be no leaving the facility for Ian for the next several months. After that, he was looking at the possibility of several years in state prison, based on several felony charges for which he had yet to be tried.

I'd devoted my life to my children, using every school, psychological service, medication—everything to save my brilliant, beautiful boy. This relentless frenzy to save his life was about a mother's love, I told myself. But now Ian was beyond my reach. I had finally come to the end of my illusion. I couldn't fix him, no matter how much I pleaded. This was PhD level parenting, far beyond the "star charts," beyond rewards and punishments, beyond grounding and taking away privileges. I had no more parenting books to read. They'd never had the chapter about my son, anyway. I could no longer advocate for Ian; this wasn't school, trying to get a teacher to understand my "spirited child." Now we'd come to the end of the line.

The workhouse was the biggest timeout ever. It was my timeout, too. The only one left to fix was me. The only place left to go was into the darkest recesses of myself, into my deepest fears. If the measure of my success was happy, thriving children, then clearly I was failing at my life's work. But this logic proved to be arrogant when I followed it further. If they were doing well, as Kate was, it would stand to reason by the same logic that I could take credit for that. With growing clarity, I learned one of the most humbling lessons of parenting: I could no more take credit for my daughter's success than take the blame for my son's predicament.

This was Ian's journey. I'd been condemned and ultimately blessed to be his guide. Nothing more. Nothing less. I didn't know if I could see him in jail. I thought I might dissolve into a sobbing heap. I didn't think I was strong enough to love him and be unable to protect him simultaneously.

"There's nothing I can do for him," I said to a friend, explaining why I wouldn't visit him in jail.

"You don't have to do anything," she suggested. "Just bring God with you."

God has been a lifelong, still-getting-to-know-you process. This suggestion gave me an idea to lean into, but absolutely no guarantees. So I went, conjuring up as much as I could about God. It was March, a dirty month of white snow giving way to garbage and rot. The skeletal trees leaning haphazardly over a half-frozen pond I drove by every week for the next several months.

I always went alone, except for the God part. Marcos and I grew farther and farther apart. He had no interest in what was happening with my son. In fact, he once told me my story about Ian's improvement was boring. So, visiting Ian in jail, in a strange way, became my sanctuary. It was my private healing place, and eventually, a source of salvation for my son and me.

While Ian was getting another chance at life, I was getting another chance at parenting. And at loving.

I sat in the waiting area with all those other wives, mothers, sisters, friends, lovers, children, and an occasional man. My first thought was: *I don't belong here.* It rushed up in me proud and arrogant, like a burp I didn't have time to muffle. But as I sat there in the jail waiting room, watching children play, grandmothers sleep, friends talking, laughing, quietly crying, all races and ages and economic levels, I realized this: I belonged right there as much as everyone else in the dingy waiting area marked by smudged plastic chairs and a filthy floor. We were all there together, each of us, because we loved someone behind bars. While there are many privileges of race and economic class, in that moment, none of that mattered.

I waited my turn to see my son. After an hour, a guard shouted my name. I joined the line, and we entered a narrow hall lined with wooden stools that faced a row of inmates seated behind scratched Plexiglass. I quickly saw Ian. His hair had grown, his face stubbled with the beard of a still young man. I sat in front of him and picked up the sticky phone.

"Hi," I breathed, looking at him through smudged glass.

We both teared up. Orange is not a good color on anyone. But even through the tears and dirty glass, I could see my son's eyes, the clearest they'd been in years. There was the boy I had given birth to. There was the soul that stared out at me from the little photograph I prayed to every day. No smudged glass or crackling phone line could dim the light beginning to emanate from Ian again.

Week by week, the skeletal trees began to sprout leaves. The garbage swept away into a full-blown spring. I became friendly with some of the people in the waiting room. I found angels there. I may have been an angel to one or two others as they waited to see their sons, husbands, or brothers. Each week, through the dirty Plexiglass, I watched Ian's body growing stronger, more vital. He'd flash his growing biceps, careful not to let the other inmates see him flex.

I had not given up on my son. I'd surrendered. And in that surrender, I began to heal, reveling in the person Ian was becoming, getting back in some ways the years we had missed. Strangely, I began to look forward to visiting him. Jail had become my hallowed ground. In many ways, jail was his church, too. He gained some forty pounds in the months he was there, growing to a proper, but still slim, weight by the time he was released several months later.

While Ian was there, gaining his wits as he gained weight, he realized the people he'd long emulated on the outside were following a path that would land them behind bars for years. As Ian became clear-headed, he knew without a doubt that jail was not what he wanted for his future. Though he still faced multiple felonies a judge had yet to sentence him for—possibly four years in state prison—Ian was ready to do everything in his power to avoid it.

Ian, his father, the lawyer, and I crowded into a tiny room before the hearing. The lawyer turned to me. "I had no idea that *you* were the tough-love person. You were the one who locked your son out of the house and changed the locks when he was using drugs."

"Yes," I said. "Finally, after years of Al-Anon, I knew this was the highest form of love."

The lawyer took off his reading glasses and looked directly at me. "And how do you know now that this time is different? How do you know that Ian is done with his old way of life?"

"Because I am the one who locked him out and changed the locks. I'm not afraid to do what I need to do when he is using. I am not in denial. I just see something—feel something—very different than what I saw before. This is different." My son and former husband nodded in agreement, both of them with eyes full of tears.

The lawyer gave me a quick, firm nod. With that, we went into court. The lawyer told the court that I was the one who had in the past stood up against Ian's addiction, and that this time I felt it was different. I quietly sobbed, moved by hearing my story in public. The strength that it took to let my first-born child go to the streets, to build a belief in a Higher Power from the flat earth of a spiritless childhood—to hear this in court was overwhelming. It was as though my parenting, as much as my son's behavior, was on trial. It was the first time in this difficult journey that I felt truly seen. Whatever happened now was out of my hands, but all of my struggles had been witnessed. The judge, a

Black woman in her fifties, lowered her reading glasses and looked past court reporters and lawyers to me as I sniffled and tried to gain my composure. Woman to woman. She pushed her glasses back up on the bridge of her nose.

"I think you have a bright future," she said to Ian. "Here's what I'm going to do: I'm going to put those three felonies up on a shelf, adjudicate them. If you break the law in any way—even a speeding ticket—those felonies will come down and go straight to sentencing. You are looking at four to five years in state prison."

As Ian finished out the last days of his sentence in the workhouse, I sold the house I'd raised my children in, hoping it would be easier for Marcos and me to start fresh and not live in the house of my former marriage. I bought a condo across the street from our studio. I cried and blessed each room in the house, thanking it for being a beautiful dwelling on a treelined street where my children had a sweet childhood. While I packed the house, Marcos camped out at a Starbucks, where he studied the American Dream by reading *The Four-Hour Work Week*.

Marcos never unpacked his clothes from the garbage bags he used for suitcases. They lived in closets, as though he were just waiting for me kick him out once again. Sure enough, I did. Marcos continued to use his weapons of withdrawal, until I asked him to leave one more time. This time there were no flowers. I asked him to leave. This time he shrugged and said, "I think I will move out."

I was shocked. My friends gently asked if Marcos could have been looking for a ticket to the US all along. I had not considered that he was using our relationship to get into the US. As I reeled with the possibility that I'd been knowingly used, each time I saw Ian, something deep inside me began to come back into alignment. Something far beyond my shame at having been taken by a handsome cad in Rome. The saddest part about the marriage ending was losing the studio I had built.

While my relationship with my son healed week by week, Marcos worked step-by-step to threaten my pre-marital assets if I did not leave him the studio with all the equipment I'd procured through a home equity line of credit and the help of my mother. I offered to give him half of the equipment or buy him out, but he dug in.

Two days after Marcos moved out, Ian moved into my condo, electronic monitoring cuff on his ankle.

Ian and I had one of the best years of our lives together as mother and son. He was sober. We were both dating, until he met the woman he would marry. We were both free—he of the confines of jail and addiction and me of the self-imposed limitations of unworthiness.

A couple of months later, as I was finalizing what I thought would be a straightforward divorce, Marcos threatened to go after premarital assets, including my retirement from my first marriage and money I made from selling my home of twenty years. He also threatened to ask for spousal maintenance if I did not give him the entire studio with all the equipment, which I'd bought with my home equity line of credit. My lawyer said these claims wouldn't hold up. In fact, he said I had a good case for marital fraud. But by the time I fought these claims, he warned, I'd be out more money than the studio and all the equipment was worth. "Run. Don't walk," the lawyer said. "Close this up. Walk away from the equipment before he gets any more crazy ideas."

Ian was there when I listened to Marcos telling me he would go after it all if I didn't walk away. To have Ian sober and present for my pain was a full circle moment that almost made up for the shock and shame I felt at letting a man take almost everything from me. Almost. I went into the fetal position, at first holding on to the wrong lessons.

As I licked my wounds, I believed:

- I can't trust anyone.
- True love doesn't exist.
- I am a fool.

Note: Ian is now in his mid-thirties, married, and a father to two beautiful children. More than ten years later, he has remained law abiding. Ian also has a very successful career—not despite his trials but *because* of them. He faced darkness and came out with a lightsaber. He chose life, and I am grateful every day he did.

WHAT I LEARNED

> "I forgive myself and set myself free."
>
> — Louise Hay

Soon word spread throughout the community—a fitness community I hadn't realized I was a part of until then. Many reached out and offered support. Within weeks, my clients came to my condo, which was just across the street from the studio Marcos now tried to run by himself. A few of my clients and my mother gave me gifts and no-interest loans to buy new equipment. By spring, I'd found a new place. I called it Embody Minneapolis. To be fully in one's body is to be fully alive. Embody became the biggest specialized fitness studio in the Twin Cities.

One after the other, my clients and other fitness trainers and owners told me in different ways my reputation was stellar, that what I did mattered, that I helped people grow and connect to themselves. That is how I began to trust again. The outpouring of love was humbling and pointed me in the right direction, helping me learn:

1. I am an entrepreneur.
2. Some people lack empathy. Believing in the essential goodness of our fellows is not a weakness.
3. Many people love me and want to see me succeed.
4. I am worthy of true love. I am worthy.

One more thing I learned: When there is nothing left to do, there is only love. Love is where forgiveness lives. This is perhaps the greatest gift of all. I revel not in the illusion I saved my son, but in the greater gift of being his and Kate's mother, for the opportunity to work on myself during his jail time, readying myself to receive the bright young man who'd emerge from jail, for the chance to face my greatest fears in the starkest way, and for being finally brought to my knees.

SELF-CARE DISCOVERY EXERCISES

1. What was the worst mistake you ever made? What did you learn?

   _____
   _____
   _____
   _____
   _____
   _____
   _____
   _____

2. What gifts did the worst situations in your life give you?

3. Have you forgiven yourself?

4. Recall a time when letting go was the only answer. What was the result of letting go?

5. How have your biggest challenges been your spiritual ground?

6. How much credit or blame do you take for other people's choices?

_____

_____

_____

_____

_____

_____

_____

_____

TIPS FOR FORGIVING YOURSELF

1. Listen to how you're talking to yourself. What's your tone? Are you calling yourself names? Stop.

2. If you were your own kind parent, what would you say about your "mistake"? Do that.

3. How different would a situation have turned out if you had exercised self-compassion?

4. What shame do you still hold onto? Look at it, and let it go.

5. Where have you or do you feel imprisoned? How can you break free?

6. Where are your angels? Look for them.

SUMMARY

> "F-E-A-R has two meanings: 'Forget Everything And Run' or 'Face Everything And Rise.' The choice is yours."
>
> — Zig Ziglar

I'd lost a husband and gained a son. I began to understand that not knowing myself and not having compassion for myself were what made me vulnerable to a narcissist and the associated dangers. I believed I wasn't enough to be worthy of a great love unless I worked for it, paid for it, and was ever vigilant in hanging on to it. I now see that falling under Marcos' spell was one of the greatest gifts of my life. I learned not loving myself was the most dangerous thing of all.

Little by little, I returned to living—wide-eyed, humbled, and much smarter. Best of all, I did not allow the lessons from my second marriage to be the wrong ones. Instead, I discovered what lives inside me. We all possess qualities that cannot be given or taken away by another.

My humility was hard-won. But it identifies me as part of the human race.

We don't make mistakes—we only learn and have Big Lessons. I challenge you to take inventory of your "mistakes" and ensure you don't squander them on the wrong lessons. I challenge you to forgive yourself by finding self-compassion. The greatest lessons come with love. I challenge you to make loving yourself your first priority. No one can give you that—and no one can take it away. I challenge you to be fearless in facing the shame that still lives in your closet. Take it out, dust it off, and send it away. Shame is the biggest impediment to growth. I challenge you to see the most challenging times as opportunities to let go of what you cannot control. Letting go takes faith. Faith is a muscle; strengthen it by exercising it. There is no other way. Faith begets faith. Courage begets courage.

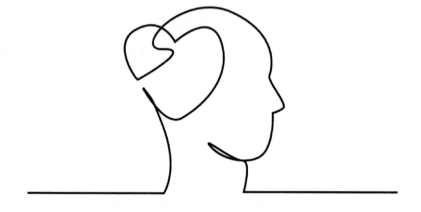

CHAPTER 11

RECEIVING THE GIFTS OF ALZHEIMER'S

"Not all mourning happens after bereavement—for some, grief can start years before the death of a loved one."

— The Conversation, theconversation.com

A year or so before my mother's death, I sat beside her in her close room, the shades drawn against the August heat in Minneapolis. Outside, I knew the lake was glistening. Birds were resting. Mom was comfortably reclined in her Cadillac of wheelchairs she had got as soon as she began losing enough weight to trigger hospice care. She was a wisp of her former body, light as a feather. When I was a young girl, I used to sit beside her while she read, playing with the veins that flowed like blue rivers beneath her luminous, soft skin.

That was how I got close to my mom: while she was reading. She allowed me to touch her in a curious, almost clinical way. She never tried to stop me, never accused me of wanting too much attention. It was a moment of silent intimacy, one not afforded us often, because she was awkward with closeness. She never said "I love you" to her children. Only, "I am very fond of you." I learned young that touching her hands with gentle curiosity was a way into her heart.

Now she was folded in on herself, lost in her dementia, unable to speak. She lived in the mysterious depths of Alzheimer's. I approached her bed slowly, careful not to startle her. "Hi, Mom. Hi, Mom," I said in a sing-song voice. She tilted her head toward the sound of my voice, like a bird, blinking her rheumy-blue eyes, her hand folded tightly against her breastbone. I touched one of her fingers, and suddenly, like a bird taking flight, she opened all her fingers, taking my hand, pressing it to her chest. It was such a small thing, and I was used to receiving small things from her, love rationed, always vigilant against spoiling me, even when I was a little girl but this tiny gesture threatened to undo me.

Years ago, I made a promise to my mother that was also, I realize now, a promise to the universe. It was in the parking lot of a clothing store in my hometown of Berkeley. She was doing her pseudo-psychological projecting that had, by my mid-forties, become part of our unique mother-daughter landscape.

"I know it's hard for you to deal with your father and me aging," she said.

"No," I said. "It's not. Because you and Dad are doing great, are active, and taking care of yourselves."

Slowly, the underlying fear began to worm its way out. She admitted she had barely visited her mother, who had suffered from Alzheimer's, in the final years before her death. My mother stopped short of saying she felt badly about that. But I comforted myself believing she did.

"I'm sorry you are struggling with that regret, Mom. But I promise you, when the time comes, I will not let you or Dad suffer. I don't know what that looks like, but I will not leave you."

Within the decade, my father died of Parkinson's, which seemed to enflame the dementia smoldering for years in my mother. I spent the next three years trying to move my mother to Minnesota from the Bay Area. The tiny kitchen in her "luxury" Oakland apartment had become a place to lay papers so she could remember what she needed to do. It was her to-do list expanded. Cooking lived there no longer.

I finally had to trick her into coming here to Minnesota. My therapist at the time called it "therapeutic fibbing." Making a decision completely against your parents' wishes—even in their best interest—is one of the most heartbreaking things a child will ever have to do. Leaving her at her first memory care facility, where the doors were locked, was far worse than leaving your young child crying at a preschool you know also has their best interest at heart. For months, my mother would get on the elevator with small groups, trying to escape her comfortable but unfamiliar new home. She would pack her suitcase and wait for imaginary friends and relatives to pick her up and drive her to the airport. She eventually settled in, but I cried nearly every time I left her, wiping my tears as I freely rode the elevator and walked freely back out and into my life.

When Mom couldn't remember anything anymore, she still knew one thing: She loved my red rain boots. She loved them again and again. Each moment brought a new opportunity to see them for the first time. Her eyes would travel from my face to my feet. "Oh," she'd say, "I love those red boots." She no longer talked about how I hadn't visited her—even if I had just come to see her the week before. It was now beauty she fixated on. Over and over, she loved my red boots.

I bought her a pair of her own red rain boots in size six-and-a-half. She was like a proud eight-year-old in those boots, her smile beaming, her double-jointed knees bending backward as they had, I'm sure, since she could walk. She still went outside with me back then. An itinerate walker, a lover of nature, I'd take her out to the path across from her memory care center. We'd take in the birds and the tall grasses. She never missed a flower or a bird. Now she had her own red rain boots, flashing red with each step she took.

I knew she was no longer being cared for at her memory care facility when I found her boots stuffed up on a high shelf in her closet. I took them down and put them on the closet floor again where she could see them every day. The next time I came, they were back on a shelf, buried beneath clothing that had floated around the facility with other residents' names sewn into the collars. I lost sleep knowing she was being attended to by people who didn't know her. They did not know she loved those red boots, so I knew they did not love her.

I moved her to a new facility on Cedar Lake in Minneapolis with trees visible from every window. During the move, I needed a break, so I took her to Target to pick up a few things. I worried about her falling, so I asked her to hold my hand. She resisted like a toddler. "I don't need to hold your hand!"

"What if I want to hold your hand, Mom?"

She looked at me suspiciously, and then reluctantly took my hand. We walked across the parking lot, my mother impossibly smaller than she'd already been. When we reached the automatic doors she turned to me. "We've come full circle," she said.

"What?" I asked, incredulous that this woman who'd disassociated my entire life, sometimes not recognizing me even as a child, for this one fleeting moment might grasp the enormity of where we were in this Target parking lot.

"You're taking care of me now," she said. "Thank you."

That was six years before her death. I thought then, *If this is the last cogent thing she says to me, I am complete.* It turned out it was. Almost. Alzheimer's disease is truly the Long Goodbye. But in many ways, my goodbye started long before she was relegated to memory care.

Over the next six years, I visited her, sometimes multiple times a week and sometimes only monthly. My favorite way to get there was through Theodore Wirth Regional Park. I'd put it in maps, allowing me to pay attention to the sights along the way. Oh, yes, I'd remember, I turn here on the parkway, past the Eloise Butler Wildflower Garden, where I'd take Mom in her red boots when she was still walking.

One time, in the glorious fall, we walked along the path in the dappled light. The path got wider, and as I held her hand with my left, I could feel my dad's in my right. They both loved being in nature. Our vacations were not car camping, but strapping packs to our little backs and hiking into the Sierra Nevada Wilderness. So, it was fitting that I found my dad's spirit beside us in those gentle woods.

I'd read Mom poetry, mostly Mary Oliver. This was how I learned to be in the silence with my mother. This is how I learned to trust that our souls were doing their own thing, convening, being mother and daughter, or some other relationship entirely from another lifetime. Sometimes I would turn away to cry, not so much with the sadness of loss, but with the poignancy of Mary Oliver's words floating between us.

Mom mostly stared blankly. On a good day, she'd close her eyes while I read, and then open them as soon as I finished. She'd nod sagely, as if there were no dementia, and I would read another poem. I believe our souls convened over poetry. Over years of tangles between us, poetry was the final elixir, the unknotting of disappointment. Just a week before her final parting, though I did not know it then, I read to her one last time.

Mom died on April 7, 2024. She was ninety-one. She was at peace— her face without worry or fear, her skin as smooth as a newborn, death erasing all the complexities her mind had held fast to. To say Alzheimer's was a gift would be a dishonor to what, especially at first, must have been a terrifying loss of memory, losing her place in what Mary Oliver called "the family of things." But for us, along with poetry, Alzheimer's was a return to the essence of what it meant to be mother and child; it was a chance for our souls to rise up and communicate as they had, perhaps, when I was a newborn and even when she was a newborn.

Alzheimer's is off-roading, beyond linear time, into deep, pathless woods, beyond speech. Mom's Alzheimer's was a reckoning, a map back to what truly matters.

One day, while driving to see Mom, taking the back way past the wildflower garden, I realized I didn't need the map anymore. I turned off the GPS. "End of route," the screen read. I drove past Cedar Shore and remembered how fast Cedar Lake came up. I will have a memorial for Mom in that wildflower garden, I thought then and know now. The sign for her facility is hidden by thick foliage in the late summer. It was the first time I ever really knew how to get to her from all directions: on the highway, through the park, or along the backroads from my condo. I finally know all the roads that lead to Mom.

Just a week before she died, I bought my mom a couple of new outfits: comfy pants and easy on-off tops. One of Mom's Kenyan caregivers asked me to get them. He said her current clothes were too difficult for the staff to get on her. "She doesn't need that drama," he said, laughing a deep laugh I will miss along with my mom.

I took away the ill-fitting clothes, removing the only drama Mom had left. I also took the red boots, knowing she didn't know or care what was in her closet anymore. At first, I carried them in the backseat of my car, thinking I'd consign them. Now her red boots are back inside my bedroom, reminding me of her love of red, our walks, and the small ways I was able to make her happy.

WHAT I LEARNED

"To live in this world

you must be able

to do three things:

> to love what is mortal;
>
> to hold it
>
> against your own bones knowing
>
> your own life depends on it;
>
> and, when the time comes to let it go,
>
> let it go."
>
> — Mary Oliver

It's taken me nearly sixty-two years to circle back to Mom, to the primacy of being her daughter. The compass of awe and gratitude has always been steering me; it comes with the amazing gift of being born—one in 400 quadrillion chances, some scientists say. My gratitude for her sacrifice has always outweighed any struggles we had. I've finally learned my way here, through the woods, over highways and backroads through the aliveness of nature, just in time to say thank you and goodbye once again.

I showed up as the daughter I wanted to be. I decided in that parking lot some twenty years ago that I was going to be the person I could live with for the rest of my years. This I accomplished. I showed up for my mother with the intention of "never letting her suffer." We do not always have control over whether other people suffer. I was lucky enough for my mother and the universe to comply, allowing me to keep my bold promise.

Mom was not always loving—sometimes cold. Her love was measured. "I am very fond of you," she'd say—and even then, only in response to me being upset about something. Though my parents did not say, "I love you" to their children, they did say it daily to each other. So, they knew how. And they felt love. It was too painful to conclude that they just didn't love us. I made up other stories instead: Saying "I love you" to us would spoil us; they thought of love as only romantic in nature, etc. In the end, my answers never quite added up, leaving me with a lasting lesson: Do not expect unconditional love. You must constantly earn it.

But something bigger than this subtle emotional neglect also always existed. I was awed by the miracle that—despite Mom's ambivalence about wanting me—I got to be *here*, on the planet. From the time I was eight years old, I was awestruck by the mysteries of life on planet earth: the clouds in the sky, nature's technicolor, the way music could make me cry. Though my family was decidedly not religious, I have always felt the spiritual swoon of gratitude and the sense that I belonged to something far bigger than myself: nameless, powerful, and beautiful. I set out to make the most of it.

Even when, or perhaps especially when, my mother was not the loving parent I yearned for, she taught me many things, including:

1. How to be my own parent.

2. How to be the daughter I wanted to be and love my mother unconditionally.

3. How to be a deep listener, even when nothing is being said.

4. How to be the mother I did not have to my own children. "You broke the cycle, Mom," my thirty-one-year-old daughter recently said as she held her first child.

SELF-CARE EXERCISES

1. What negative generational cycles have you set out to break?

   _____
   _____
   _____
   _____
   _____
   _____
   _____
   _____
   _____
   _____

2. What has incurable illness—either in yourself or someone you love—taught you?

   _____
   _____
   _____
   _____
   _____
   _____
   _____

3. Describe how you want people to remember you.

   _____
   _____
   _____
   _____
   _____
   _____
   _____
   _____

4. Reflect on your regrets. Are there wrongs you'd like to right? What are you doing about it?

___

5. Anticipatory grief can get in the way of being present to the joy right here, right now. Write about a situation you are already grieving even though the person is still alive. Is grief getting in the way of enjoying them now?

___

6. It is possible to make up for the deficits of our ancestors by creating a legacy of abundance. What does your legacy look like?

_____

_____

_____

_____

_____

_____

_____

TIPS FOR SPEAKING SOUL

1. Read poetry aloud. Ideally to someone with whom you'd like to connect.

2. Be with a baby or an elderly person regularly. If they want to talk, talk. But learn to be present in silence too. This is a gift to others.

3. Imagine your soul actively seeking other souls. What healing and reconciliation might be going on beneath your thinking mind?

4. What gifts can you give that were not given to you?

SUMMARY

> "We are blessed.
> Each day is a chance.
> We have two arms.
> Fear wastes air."
>
> — Mark Nepo

To hold my mother's hand in a parking lot and read to her while she dozed was to regain a sweetness I must have once had with her before I could speak. To "come full circle," as my mother recognized for that fleeting moment at the entrance of Target, was at once a healing, forgiveness, and a reconciliation I did not think was possible. In fact, I did not know how deeply I yearned for it still.

While I missed Mom deeply as she lost herself layer by layer to Alzheimer's, I had been missing her long before the disease took her presence from me, leaving her body while taking her personality. Yet along with much of her personality, Alzheimer's also took her grudges. She could no longer nurse resentments because she couldn't hang onto them. Memory helps us retain good things, but it also helps us nurse our negative stories. Alzheimer's is not discerning. Mom lost it all. Each time I went to see her, rather than berate me for not seeing her more often, she thanked me and told me how lovely it was to see me—whether it had been a day or a month. In this way, my mother taught me how to be in the moment, too.

As Mom lost her words, she became my Zen teacher. This was when I learned to let my soul talk. My soul reached out and touched her soul. I imagined somewhere on a plane beyond time and the roles assigned to us during this life, I was perhaps her mother in another. Or we were beyond all of those roles, and we were just two souls keeping each other company for a while, as we rode the poetry bus together until her body once and finally died.

Regret is a way to hold onto an old story. It is a way to combat the fear that life might be different or it can be different. I challenge you to let go of regret. It is a soul-sucker. I challenge you to love with all your heart—even loving those who have not been able to love you. To love without conditions is to heal your own heart. I challenge you to break the cycle that has not served you and create one that does. I challenge you to create a new legacy, starting right now.

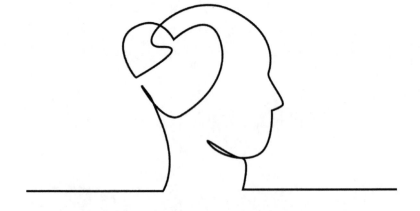

CHAPTER 12

FALLING IN LOVE WITH YOURSELF

"When love beckons to you, follow him,

Though his ways are hard and steep.

And when his wings enfold you yield to him,

Though the sword hidden among his pinions may wound you.

And when he speaks to you believe in him,

Though his voice may shatter your dreams as the north wind lays waste the garden.

For even as love crowns you so shall he crucify you. Even as he is for your growth so is he for your pruning.

Even as he ascends to your height and caresses your tenderest branches that quiver in the sun,

So shall he descend to your roots and shake them in their clinging to the earth.

Like sheaves of corn he gathers you unto himself

He threshes you to make you naked.

He sifts you to free you from your husks.

He grinds you to whiteness.

He kneads you until you are pliant;

And then he assigns you to his sacred fire, that you may become sacred bread for God's sacred feast.

All these things shall love do unto you that you may know the secrets of your heart, and in that knowledge become a fragment of Life's heart."

— Kahlil Gibran

I dove into dating the way I attended grad school. I believed I'd skipped an essential step in my development. Maybe dating was like crawling before you walk, I reasoned your brain doesn't develop correctly if you don't pass through a knee-banging, awkward, and essential strength-building phase. I needed to go through that dating, even if I was forty-five, not seventeen. I'd skipped it because I believed dating only opened me up to misunderstandings, sullying my "reputation," and possible sexual assault. Plus, I have always hated small talk. Having a "real" monogamous boyfriend, I believed, was the only way to have an authentic, trusting connection. But maybe I'd missed something.

To find the right partner—read, *not make a mistake again*—I was going to have practice. My main school was Match.com. I sifted through dozens of profiles, skimming for the essentials first: age, education, and the most obvious: whether they could write English reasonably well. I posted the best pictures of myself that Kate had taken of me in Italy. I thought I was off to a good start with one of my first dates.

"Do you like to cook?" the handsome man asked.

The restaurant was small and softly lit as dusk settled over the Minneapolis street outside. It was early summer when in Minnesota the weather gives us unbounded hope. But even at the peak of summer when we've almost forgotten what the landscape looks like with leafless trees, we still know winter always comes. I so wanted a partner by the time the snow flew, someone to curl up with on the couch and keep each other company through the darkness.

"Yes, I love to cook!" I said. This was one of the first dates in my dating phase, and it was typical of what happened on many dates. I'll call this man "Steve."

"What's your favorite thing to cook?" Steve asked.

"I'm an intuitive cook," I told him, missing my chance to show off my signature dish and thereby convince him I was a "good" cook. But perhaps this would launch us onto a more interesting and less travelled path away from his checklist. I pictured him putting a mental sad face by the cooking question. Then he moved on.

"What else are you good at?" he asked.

"Well, I'm really intuitive," I said, brightly, still painfully hoping.

"Oh, yeah?" he leaned in now. "Can you read me?"

I shifted a bit in my seat, which was beginning to feel very hard. "I don't know," I said.

"Read me," Steve insisted. "Go on. Read me."

I looked out the window of the restaurant I'd always loved, wanting more than anything not to scare this man away. Was I hesitating because I feared I might not read him correctly? No, that wasn't it. I was afraid I *would* read him correctly. But the interview didn't seem to be helping me anyway, so I turned on my intuition light.

Bringing my gaze back from the darkening street, I looked deeply into Steve's eyes. "I think you've been hurt a lot, and you're really scared. I think this line of questioning comes from that fear."

He looked stricken.

"Should I go on?" I asked.

"No," he said. "That's enough."

The interview was over. The dishes were cleared; the check was brought. We took a little walk and wandered aimlessly through a used bookstore. (I think this was also on his checklist.) We hugged goodnight. I knew I would not be seeing him again. I turned over in my head everything I might have done wrong, concluding I was too much and to keep it light from now on. *You can do this*, I reasoned. *Just keep it light.*

Could I actually tackle dating lightly? Though the *idea* had always sounded fun, it rarely was for me. Dating was more than a full-time job. It was a mission that often demanded contorting myself—a practice in being authentic, but also being what you think the other person is looking for. I realize now it is impossible to be both yourself and be someone else. But no one tried harder to do the impossible and maintain a positive attitude.

No matter how light I tried to keep it, more than one date exclaimed, "Wow, you're so deep." They did not say it in a complimentary way. It was as though I'd turned on my high beams, and they felt they were being searched.

I was mystified. Ian, wearing an electronic ankle bracelet, was living with me now. For the first time in years, he was clean and sober, working and dating. Together, we were having one of the best years of our entire relationship. To witness your children thriving, whether they're two or twenty-five or fifty, is a joy like no other. To share this strange time with my son, who also happens to be very deep, psychic, and whip smart, was a gift I never even knew to wish for.

"Men keep saying I'm deep," I said as Ian and I sat in the living room. Soon it would be cold enough outside to use the fireplace. "Even when I'm just talking about the weather, they think I'm deep. I can't imagine how they'd feel if I actually talked about something important. I don't get it. I'm trying so hard to not be deep."

"Oh, Mom," Ian said, "you *are* deep. You can't help it. It's like your soul reaches up and touches their soul while you're just sitting there having a conversation. They're not ready to have their souls touched."

Hearing this was a relief. It wasn't my fault! I couldn't help but be deep. I was born with this soul-touching thing. Like being an introvert or an extrovert, I was a soul-toucher. Now, when I saw my date retreating from the light, I blamed myself a little less. He just wasn't ready to have his soul touched.

Other times, the man was clearly ready to have his soul touched. Or to be touched at all. *We're all so lonely*, I thought many times in my dating career. We're all just out here trying to be seen and heard, to be loved for who we are. One man bravely cut out a heart in an avocado half and took a photo of it beside a note on construction paper that said, "I love you." We'd gone on two or three dates and, being a good listener, he'd learned I loved avocados. Though he himself had never eaten an avocado, he was so selfless he bought one and turned it into a crafty representation of his love for me.

"I have something for you," he said, as we sat across from each other at a restaurant. As he reached into his pocket, I was flooded with fear. His wife had died three years before, and he wanted more than anything to end this single pause and go back to being mated for life. To my great relief, he pulled out his phone, not a box.

"Here," he said mischievously, "I'll text it to you."

I opened my phone to the photo of the avocado, slightly browned, the pit missing, the heart shape in its place sitting beside the words, "I love you."

"Oh," I said, trying to take it all in, while searching for the appropriate response.

"It's an avocado," he said, excitedly. "That's a heart!"

"I see that," I said. "Wow, that's so sweet."

I felt slightly nauseous as we ate our dinner. A few days later, I called him.

"I'm going to release you," I said, "so you can find a woman who loves you the way you deserve to be loved."

Later, he sent me a note thanking me for my "class" and "honor."

He was a good one.

Some dates seemed serious enough to take my profile down. These periods of three or four months were welcome respites from the algorithmic pressure of Match. But in my desperation to find a man and end my search for love, I compromised my values—and sometimes my safety. Aaron was a six-foot-four, stylish, seemingly easy-going man a few years my junior. He treated me like a "lady" in public, opening doors, paying the bill with easy confidence. In private, he bought me clothes and groomed me to be his naughty playmate. The pressure was constant.

I played along to a point for a bit. But it soon became clear Aaron was a dirty drunk who cleaned himself up for me. His apartment was dirty and stale. His bathroom was filthy. The entryway was broken down. His car was nice, but it had an ignition interlock device, also known as a car breathalyzer, required by the state due to his DUIs. When I finally mentioned the breathalyzer to Ian, he said matter-of-factly, "Oh, so he's an alcoholic." I sputtered and made excuses the same way Aaron used to.

"It's okay, Mom. Lots of great people are alcoholics," he said, reassuringly.

When Aaron popped me in the cheek in a drunken twitch in the middle of the night, that was it. Something snapped. I was not then nor ever would be in love with Aaron. The facts—he was dishonest and his first love was drinking—overshadowed all his sweet talk. But he didn't let me go easily. He launched a steady stream of gaslighting, obfuscation, manipulation, begging, and promises. This went on long enough for me to begin to doubt myself. I bemoaned the situation to my coach at the time:

"What's wrong with me that I can't let this nice man love me?" I asked.

"What's *right* with you that you can't stay in a relationship where the central player is alcohol?" she said.

I asked myself: "Why did I carry on with a sick person for months? Why didn't I leave sooner?" This is the central question of my dating life. This was part of my answer, revealed in therapy: My father taught me how to sit at the table with crazy. Mom's craziness always had a place at our white Formica table. No one was allowed to call it out. My father and I chattered on, as Mom talked to herself looking into her food, and my brother ate slowly and steadily in dreamy silence. I was accustomed to things not making sense and everyone around me acting like nothing was wrong. This gaslighting helped me deny things like alcoholism, narcissism, and manipulation in all cases.

I had a Match date with someone named Jay whose handle was "Casanova," and his status was "separated." These should have been red flags, but I hadn't quite gotten my high school attraction to bad boys out of my system.

"Too bad you're still married," I wrote, "and that you're a Casanova."

"You have the wrong impression of me. I'm not married, and Casanova is my dog's name."

"Must be a sexy dog," I responded.

I went out with him anyway. He was smooth, mysterious, and drove a nice car. I'm a sucker for nice cars. But it soon became apparent, by his mostly unfurnished downtown apartment, he was married.

Then, there was the Buddhist who went on silent retreats and posted on Instagram about his gratitude practice. Early in the relationship, he wanted me to meet his teenage daughters. I was flattered but told him we should probably wait a bit. He took me to a restaurant a ways out of the city. When we were finally seated, a waitress recognized him. It turned out she thought I was his ex. He did not correct her or introduce me.

He posted pictures of what he was grateful for, while apparently not seeing what was right in front of him. On Instagram, he gushed about someone else taking photos of flowers at a gas station. "Pick me! Pick me! I am those flowers at the gas station," I silently begged. Soon, I began to get cynical. "You are so busy hunting around for things you're grateful for that you're not attending to the most present good thing in your life," I journaled. "You're too busy forcing things that aren't meant to be."

I had an eight-month relationship with Joe, the father of one of Ian's best friends from middle school. I'd always thought Joe was very handsome in an elegant-goofy way that disarmed me and made me want to take care of him. It turned out his family saw me as an angel because I'd come into his life after he'd made a devastatingly reckless investment in stock futures. He was suicidally depressed as he watched his tens of thousands of dollars drain away. He jokingly told me to "keep an oar in the water." I had no idea this had been a pattern in his life—making tons of money and losing it as he tried to keep up and keep face with his wealthy friends.

Being one of the top sellers in his insurance consortium earned Joe two tickets for a boutique concierge cruise along the coast of Spain and Morocco. One night, as we sailed through the Strait of Gibraltar, I awoke to him standing in front of an open window, the wind howling in, the sea rising and falling violently in the dark. He braced himself with his hands on the walls of the elegant cabin while the thrashing sea and wild wind threatened to pull him away from civilization once and for all.

"Oh my God, Joe!" I screamed over the roar. "What are you doing? Close the window!"

He just stood there bracing himself for another minute, clearly enjoying the danger and the wildness.

He finally came back to bed, telling me everything was fine. I barely slept the rest of the night lying next to a man who seemed to feel most alive in the face of danger and risk as the ship was tossed around on our way to Casablanca.

One day, Joe said, "I'm going to marry you, Susan Gaines," and he created his own blueprints for remodeling his condo. He literally gave me a picture of happily-ever-after with increased closet space. But the next day, he ignored me, watching the Sunday morning news with a stony expression on his face.

In a final face-off, I asked Joe why he'd quit doing all the things that made him feel better—therapy, anti-depressants, and yoga, to name the big ones. He said he just didn't feel like it. I pointed out that we seemed to be having a rougher time since he'd quit those practices. Gently at first, I asked him to recommit to our relationship by getting back into therapy, but he refused on the grounds that I was "forcing him."

"Get back to therapy or throw in the towel," I repeated gently, resolutely. I was a one-person intervention. In the end, the disease won.

"I'm going to throw in the towel," Joe said. The tableau of him standing perfectly calm in the dark as the wind howled and the sea churned through the Strait of Gibraltar came back to me. I moved my cat and a couple pieces of furniture back to my condo and stayed there licking my wounds, recovering from one of the most exhilarating and bruising relationships of my "mature" life.

Journal entry: "I broke up with a man who gave me an avocado pitted in the shape of a heart—though he'd never eaten an avocado and, until his art project declaring his love, he didn't know they had pits. I broke up with one man because he had an affair. I broke up with another because he was a narcissist. I broke up with another because he was a sexist, racist, antisemite, disguised as a liberal. Another was an alcoholic. Another was likely bipolar, untreated. Another because he was a Buddhist practicing gratitude who was totally self-absorbed. Wanted: an avocado-eating real man who knows how to love me and appreciates how amazing I am."

But the worst was yet to come. You're never too old for date rape. I was fifty-four when I experienced it. I willingly let a man drive me in his sleek Mercedes to his house in one of Minneapolis' nicest neighborhoods—ostensibly to let his dog out. I was even attracted to him before a kiss became a frenzied disrobing. Maybe if he'd been nice to me after he pinned me down on his couch, I might have felt less traumatized. But instead, I watched in numb silence as he pulled his pants back on with perfunctory efficiency and acted as if nothing had happened. He suddenly looked at my stricken face as though seeing me for the first time.

"What's wrong with you?"

"What just happened?" I asked, trying to wrap my head around the sense of shock and violation washing over me.

I don't remember what he said. I'm not sure any answer would have sufficed or taken my shock away. The gaslight continued as he drove me home, pointing out the magical lights on the frozen lake for an annual winter carnival. I could not sleep, haunted by flashbacks of him yanking the pillow out from under my head, rendering me less comfortable and more helpless. Fortunately for me, my therapist got angry *for* me as I told her it was my fault.

"Susan," she said, "that was a sexual assault. This guy is practiced at this. He groomed you."

She witnessed me. She named the experience. Because of this, the assault did not live in me as such for long. I was not left deeply scarred by the date rape—thanks to the healers with whom I'd already surrounded myself. But it was the last time I allowed a man to share in my special gifts—emotionally, physically, or spiritually—until he was well-vetted.

Slowly, I began to call myself back. I began to take care of myself as if I were my own special child. I bought a food sealer and new cookbooks. Since I had been a child and mom had let me loose in the kitchen, making food was my healing practice. I went back to it, inhaling the warm scents of spices. I packaged and froze individual servings of restaurant quality food. Seeing the food I'd lovingly made for myself in my freezer made me feel safe and loved.

As I nourished myself, I also began meditating. I formed a practice of sitting, being with my pain and joy, with whatever was present—

loneliness, fear, sadness, love—and I slowly found a soulmate in myself. I loved being by myself in my cozy condo that winter, reading and sitting with my sweet old cat. With a great sigh of relief, I closed my dating accounts. *It's going to take a very special man for me to allow him to share this space with me*, I thought one day. *It's going to take someone who is not going to steal my serenity but enhance it.*

"You are the Jonathan Livingston Seagull of dating," my lifelong friend Thalia told me. "Each person you date represents a higher level of standards, an evolution in relationships."

I love her hopeful perspective on what feels like an assignment that has far outlasted its self-assigned purpose: to learn everything I can and finally secure a happy, healthy relationship. It's as though I'd been assigned to live on another planet, find love, and come home. "I am ready to come home—with or without love," I heard myself say.

So, I did. I came home to myself. I came home from what at first felt like a failed mission. I was still single, after all. But gradually, as I began to cherish my time alone, I had an epiphany: The mission did not fail. I had, in fact, come home with love, to love—the kind of love no one can give or take away. I am a child of the universe, "a fragment of Life's heart," as Gibran writes in *The Prophet*.

There is nothing quite like the feeling of realizing the primary love relationship you've been yearning for has been right there the whole time you thought you were exiled. As I began to forgive myself and find self-compassion for the first time since being a child when self-acceptance is a given, I was falling in love with the person in the mirror.

Finally, my higher self said, *I've been waiting for you. Welcome home.*

I put my feet up on the coffee table, ate the delicious food I'd made, and exhaled.

WHAT I LEARNED

> "After a while you learn the subtle difference
> Between holding a hand and chaining a soul,
>
> And you learn that love doesn't mean leaning
> And company doesn't mean security,
>
> And you begin to learn that kisses aren't contracts
> And presents aren't promises
>
> And you begin to accept your defeats
> With your head up and your eyes open,
>
> With the grace of a woman,
> Not the grief of a child
>
> And you learn to build all your roads on today,
> Because tomorrow's ground is too uncertain for plans

and futures have a way of falling down in mid-flight...."

— Jorge Luis Borges
(revised and copyrighted by Veronica Shoffstall)

Just after I finally understood why Joe kept saying, "Keep an oar in the water," I paddled away. I realized all the drama that seemed to follow him was of his making. But letting go of the dream is always heartbreaking. In one of the last lucid moments my mother had, she asked me, "How's your love life?"

Though I did not believe she knew exactly what she was asking, I didn't care. I overlaid the moment with the deep yearning for my mother, the one I'd lost in pieces long before the full onset of Alzheimer's, way back when I was thirteen and she told me that confiding in her was a burden. I confided in her. I told her how Joe and I had broken up. She had met him a couple of times, but whether she remembered him was not important. My eyes filled with tears, and I told her more, afraid she'd reject me as she did when I was just a girl. But she surprised me.

"Oh, I'm so sorry," she said. "I want to give you a hug."

I got up and went around to her side of the table, more to fulfill her wish than to get the love I so desperately needed. We hugged, a bit awkwardly, and then she asked, "What can I do for you, honey?"

"This is enough, Mom."

"I feel like you have a special place for me in your memory," I said hopefully. "You always know who I am."

"That is true," she said. "Without a doubt. I love you."

Just before the curtain of dementia dropped on my mother's stage, she knew me. Not only that, but after a childhood of "I'm fond of you," Mom told me she loved me. But did I know who I was? Did I love myself? If you do not know yourself, let alone love yourself, you cannot truly stand up for yourself. You are doomed to repeat the same relationship until you do.

Though I paid lip service in my journal to my worth, apparently the world had to get darker and more dangerous before I embodied self-worth. As it turns out, my initial avoidance of dating because it could leave you vulnerable to sexual assault was correct. And being "older" does not protect you from this possibility. Sexual assault can happen at any age.

Monogamously coupled at nineteen to the man I would marry at twenty-two had arrested my development in the ways of intimate relationships. When I began dating for the first time at forty-five, beginning with my second husband, I picked up where I'd left off. I looked for men who fit a "type" I developed as a teen: bad boy, lone wolf, someone to fix when he comes back to the den. Except now, as a grown woman, I also wanted him to be stable financially, love me wholeheartedly, and be vulnerable. Vulnerability and bad boy don't usually go together.

Sometimes, we must go far away on deep safaris to come back to what really matters. Everything I truly needed was right in front of me. It was within me. The experience of not being seen over and over, of trying to make myself into something I thought a man wanted, of being violated and gaslit—these were the long roads that ultimately led me home. Once I was home, I learned to cherish myself, enjoy my own company, as Borges writes, "With the grace of a woman, not the tears of a child."

SELF-CARE EXERCISES

1. Reflect on a time when you were trying to find a romantic partner. What did it teach you?

    _____
    _____
    _____
    _____
    _____
    _____

1. How has dating or long-term relationships held up a mirror for you? What did those relationships reflect?

   _____
   _____
   _____
   _____
   _____
   _____
   _____

2. When and in what ways have relationships brought you home to yourself?

   _____
   _____
   _____
   _____
   _____
   _____
   _____

3. If dating is a chapter in your life, what's it really about? Write a summary of that chapter.

_____
_____
_____
_____
_____
_____
_____

4. When do you abandon yourself in pursuit of a partnership or to maintain the one you have? Write about it.

_____
_____
_____
_____
_____
_____
_____

5. Reflect on your biggest heartbreak. What did that heartbreak teach you? What story do you tell yourself about the potential to get hurt?

_____
_____
_____
_____
_____
_____
_____

TIPS FOR FALLING IN LOVE WITH YOURSELF

1. Take yourself on a date once a week, whether it's a walk or a movie.

2. Make yourself healthy, delicious food; enjoy the sensory process.

3. Choose to be alone in your home; light a candle, put on music, or just curl up and read a book.

4. Write about all the reasons you love yourself.

5. Make a list of the qualities you want in a partner in terms of how they see and treat *you*.

SUMMARY

"…After a while you learn that even sunshine
Burns if you get too much
So you plant your own garden and decorate your own soul,
Instead of waiting for someone to bring you flowers
And you learn that you really can endure…
that you really are strong
and you really do have worth,
and you learn and learn…
With every goodbye you learn."

— Jorge Luis Borges
(revised and copyrighted by Veronica Shoffstall)

I finally learned to decorate my own soul. The next order of business was to fiercely protect my garden. In dating, I'd abandoned myself, left my soul, and then found myself bewildered when men thought I was "deep." It turned out my soul was doing its own thing—reaching out and touching other souls. Once I understood this, I was able to accept something very special about myself. I would not be a good partner for just anyone. It might take a while, I reasoned. But in the meantime, being with myself was fulfilling in a way I had never imagined.

Nothing is more vulnerable and life-changing than being in relationship with others. It is a crucial part of the human experience with the power to make us our very best. But the pursuit can leave us bereft of confidence and fearful we'll never find "the one." I challenge you to notice the story you tell yourself about dating and relationships. I challenge you to reflect daily on what makes you special—turn the story of "too much" or "not enough" into just right.

I challenge you to see where you are abandoning yourself. I challenge you to notice where and to whom you give away your power. I challenge you to make a commitment to the love of your life: you.

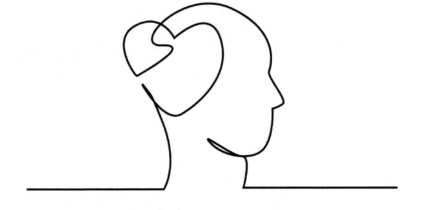

CHAPTER 13

DESIGNING YOUR RELATIONSHIP

> "Cherish your solitude. Take trains by yourself to places you have never been. Sleep out alone under the stars. Learn how to drive a stick shift. Go so far away that you stop being afraid of not coming back. Say No when you don't want to do something. Say Yes if your instincts are strong, even if everyone around you disagrees. Decide whether you want to be liked or admired. Decide if fitting in is more important than finding out what you're doing here. Believe in kissing."
>
> — Eve Ensler

I was having a drink with a friend in a trendy South Minneapolis restaurant when a tall, handsome man with a thick head of salt-and-pepper-colored hair approached our table.

"Do you write that column for *Metro Magazine*?" he asked with boyish curiosity. He was a waiter at the restaurant, but not our waiter.

"Yes," I sputtered, feeling the heat rising to my face.

"I love your column," he said before my awkwardness went on too long. "You're such a good writer. I read it every month."

For some people, food is the way to the heart. For me, it's someone who "gets" my writing—and, therefore, gets me. His compliment went straight to my heart.

"Thank you," I managed to say.

"I'm Craig," he said.

"I guess you already know my name," I said.

"It's nice to meet you," he said, grinning, and then mercifully strode away.

"How did he know who I was?" I asked my friend, blushing furiously.

"Your picture is in the magazine every month," she reminded me. "Sometimes it's full-page."

This was true. I wrote personal essays accompanied by dramatic photos of me swinging from a silk hanging from a warehouse ceiling, mountain biking, doing yoga, tai chi, boxing, and Tae Kwon Do. Each month in "Personal Gaines," I explored increasingly intimate subjects, many of which I've shared in this book. Each time I wrote, I imagined my words creating a bridge between my loneliness, my struggles to make sense of life's challenges, and those of others experiencing similar struggles. I sometimes imagined that with each piece I was calling out across a wide valley, "You're not alone. We all experience these things. I hope my story gives you hope. Maybe one day we'll meet!"

I felt a little bit famous. But more importantly, someone had heard me! And he had walked right up to my table. I felt exposed. Seen. Admired. And still quite safe. I frequented that restaurant for another several years until it closed. I was married and so was he, so that was the extent of it. If we acknowledged each other after that, it was with a vague familiarity, but no more. Sometimes I caught other people staring at me as though they might recognize me. But only Craig had the courage to walk right up to me and ask.

If you had told me that same waiter who had boldly walked up to me in a trendy restaurant while having a drink with a friend would become my life partner ten years later, I would have never believed you. But after a decade that included a quick, awful second marriage, a couple of boyfriends, and many bad dates, Craig reached out with a simple message on social media. "Hey," he wrote, "I know we don't know each other, but we could change that. Would you like to meet for a glass of wine?"

I was not accustomed to messaging through social media, so I thought the message might have been there for quite some time. I hate to keep anyone waiting. As a self-employed person, timeliness has made the difference between growing my business and letting it go to someone else. Also, I'm just afraid I'll forget, so I answer immediately—often to the shock of the recipient. After I reminded myself who he was and saw he was a father and a local actor with ties to the community, I said *yes*.

It turned out that while Craig had been thinking about asking me out for quite some time. He'd only sent his message minutes before. He was shocked by my swift response.

"Oh shit," he later recounted. "She said yes! Am I ready for that?"

He'd been living part time with his three sons in a tiny apartment, heading toward divorce. While he'd had a couple of friends set him up, this was the first time he'd made the bold move to ask out someone he did not know.

For my part, despite all the bad dates, I had not given up on love. While I was done with desperately searching, and had finally landed at home with myself and cherishing my solitude, I still believed in saying yes. Because I'd become my own soul mate, I trusted myself in the most essential ways of taking care of myself. I had healed the ultimate betrayal: the betrayal of myself. This time I brought the self-trust to the first date—and all the rest thereafter.

1. **Intuition:** I will know what I need to know, when I need to know it.

2. **Attraction:** I will trust my attraction. I can be attracted to what is safe and good.

3. **Pacing:** I can take all the time I need for each and every thing that happens between us. I will go slowly, checking in often with how I'm feeling.

With that knowledge and those commitments in my pocket, I went on a date with Craig. It was a beautiful Saturday evening in early August. The trees were fat, the air warm. The Mississippi River flowed thick and heavy just beyond the park. I didn't know then what Craig was feeling. But for once it didn't matter. What mattered was my life did not depend on how this date went or whether he liked me. I had a beautiful home waiting for me. I had a perfect home right inside me. I *was* home. That's who showed up: a woman at home in herself. I was curious, playful—and deep. Don't forget deep. Because, as my son pointed out so many years before, I can't help it.

My soul must have reached out and touched his because Craig asked me out again. And again. He planned so many creative, inexpensive, or free dates. All of them priceless. We laughed and laughed. We became friends. Really good friends. There was no one I'd rather be with. For several weeks, that's where it stayed—until we kissed goodnight, and I felt it down to my toes. I had never stopped believing in kissing either.

Dating Craig happened to coincide with the beginning of my life coaching journey. Coaching taught me how to be intentional with my life. It gave me a blueprint for "designing an alliance" with anyone and everyone with whom I work, socialize, or live. I presented the idea of designing an alliance with Craig, explaining that we could make our relationship anything we wanted. We were in charge.

First, he had some past alliances and ghosts from his marriage to clear out. He had to figure out if this thing with me was it, or whether he needed to go sow some wild oats.

"I'm done," I said. "I'm done sowing wild anything. I am not the wild sort. I am free now. No longer driven to prove my worth by other people's views of me. But if you need to go out and make a bunch of mistakes like I did, go to it."

Craig said he needed a few days to think, to write in his journal. What? A man who writes in his journal to figure things out? As secure as I'd become in my own company, the few days of him thinking threatened to upset my apple cart at least a little. I knew I could make it alone. But now I was in love with him, and I didn't want to go it alone. I chose him. Now I waited for him to choose me. He came over one day and sat me down on the couch.

"Susan," he said, taking my hand.

This is it, I thought. *Time for him to go sow his wild oats.*

"I love you. You're more than I ever imagined possible in a partner."

I waited for the "but." But it didn't come.

"I want to design an alliance with you."

Never would the words I learned in my coach training and certification with CTI (Co-Active Training Institute) sound so romantic. "I want to design an alliance with you" reminded me of the most heartfelt commitments anyone ever uttered in my direction. As I had been a dozen years before in a trendy South Minneapolis restaurant, I was speechless in the face of Craig's sureness.

"Ditto," I said, unable to find my own words.

WHAT I LEARNED

> "When someone loves you, the way they say your name is different. You know that your name is safe in their mouth."
>
> — Jess C. Scott

Five years after our first date, we moved in full-time together. Craig's son, eighteen at the time, also moved in half-time. My condo is a one bedroom, plus a windowless den. As much as this seemed like the healthy next step, I'd be lying if I said it wasn't a tiny bit hard to give up my solitude. In the frenzy of dating, I couldn't have imagined I would ever be so healed, happy, and content in my own company that I might one day be in danger of choosing my solitude over coupledom. But this was the moment. And I did miss my space. And Craig missed having a place to put his things—some place more than a pocket-doored linen closet I reluctantly cleared out for him. He may have missed more, too, but he didn't show it.

We were both trying to do it right this time. Like all couples, we were exorcising our own demons—our regrets, our wounds—and bringing in fresh angels of hope, a belief in a shared future, one not made of the romantic dreams of teenagers but the deep, abiding love of mature adults who have hurt and been hurt by others. Perhaps one of the biggest symptoms of maturity and signs of healing is the knowledge that each of us is victim and perpetrator in the game of love, that we choose, however unconsciously, the relationships we most need. We are doomed to repeat them until we learn what we need to learn.

More than a year into our cohabitation, I crave my alone time less and less, while Craig is learning to love his own company when I am not around. In each other's company, we excel, we grow, reach, and experiment. We love each other in a way that can only be described as "mature." "We get to design it," Craig often says, as though reminding us both this relationship is "human-made." It's ours. Just as we have a home for ourselves individually, this relationship has a container, too. Within that container, we cheer each other on; we ask for what we need. (That's a scary one for us both.) But intentionality is our guiding light. Intentionality *is* maturity.

SELF-CARE DISCOVERY EXERCISES

1. When have you created an understanding with someone about how you will both communicate? What were the results?

   _____

   _____

   _____

   _____

   _____

   _____

2. Do you have a relationship now with a friend or romantic partner with whom you could design an alliance? What are your hopes and fears about trying this?

   _____

   _____

   _____

   _____

   _____

   _____

3. Reflect on the meaning and purpose of coupledom. What can it teach you about your humanity?

_____

_____

_____

_____

_____

_____

_____

4. What are your beliefs about "true" love? Where were those beliefs made? Write about it.

_____

_____

_____

_____

_____

_____

_____

5. How has heartbreak shaped your view of love? What story are you carrying about the benefits and dangers of love relationships?

_____

_____

_____

_____

_____

_____

_____

TIPS FOR DESIGNING AN ALLIANCE FOR YOUR RELATIONSHIP

1. Arrange a time to design an alliance with your partner. This can even be with a new partner.

2. Ask each other what the best form of communication is. How do they best take in feedback and information?

3. Talk to each other about what shuts you down and what motivates you.

4. Ask each other how you want to be held when things are hard. Do you need time alone? Do you need reassurance?

Note: Alliances are flexible containers in which your relationship is held. They can change anytime. You can revisit your alliance weekly, annually, or whenever it needs a review and touch-up.

SUMMARY

"Real love ought to be more like a tree and less like a flower."

— Mya Robarts

"Neurons that fire together, wire together," they say in neurobiology. My anxiety and love wires were tangled. For many years, I thought constant worry that my partner would leave or was already cheating was a symptom of love. So, when anxiety was absent, I feared maybe love was too. But I soon realized if I wanted to change the sort of relationships I was attracting, I needed to disentangle that false connection between insecurity and love. Being hungry for love, fearing your partner is going to cheat or leave without warning, does not mean you love them. It only means you're desperate for them to love *you*. Being aware of this false connection was the beginning of rewiring my brain.

By the time I met Craig, I was at least ready to equate a sense of safety and security with love. Gone were the days when I would spend all my energy trying to win approval. I'd made a vow to myself if I felt that again that it was time to go. I have not felt that once with Craig. I broke the cycle of choosing men who had one foot out the door. Craig is my designed alliance guy. He is my co-designer. Craig is the guy who says my name with love and respect.

I challenge you to spend time alone so you can fall in love with yourself. If you don't love yourself, how can you expect anyone else to? I challenge you to explore how your love wires might cross. For example, notice where you may equate things like extreme jealousy with love, or fear with love. Fear is not love; it is the opposite. Which are you choosing? I challenge you to design an alliance with your partner. It's never too late. I challenge you to remember a relationship is a living, breathing thing two people create together. If it's not working, redesign it. Grow your trees. Plant your flowers. This is the garden of your relationship.

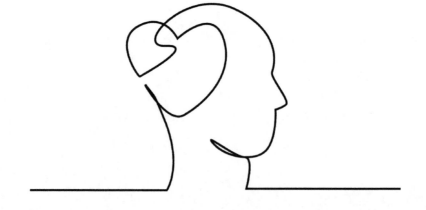

CHAPTER 14

BREATHING THROUGH PANDEMONIUM

"What lies behind us and what lies before us are tiny matters compared to what lies within us."

— Ralph Waldo Emerson

I'd just begun to really make friends with myself, to love being alone, when the world packed a one-two punch that forced the issue. First, there was pandemonium bearing different names, including COVID-19, Novel Corona Virus, and eventually The Pandemic.

I heard the rumors. Whispers. *It's coming. It's here.* A killer of epic proportions from all the way across the world. Outside, everything looked normal at first. But our cities' hospitals housed the victims of this so-far invisible war. Photos emerged from the front: exhausted healthcare workers bearing the visible scars of wearing tight N-95 masks, and the less visible scars of sadness and trauma. "Shifts" disappeared as hospital hallways became morgues. Hospitals were no longer places of healing. They became dungeons of hell, where people died without their loved ones, accompanied only by doctors and nurses who were mostly helpless in the face of an unknown killer.

Those of us in the fitness and personal care business were told to go home, to wait for further instructions. My world instantly shrank to the four walls of my condo. At first, the silence was not peaceful. The quieter it got, the louder my anxiety became. I was on high alert. Was that a sore throat? I swallowed obsessively. Was that COVID? Masking, washing groceries, holding my breath when I walked by neighbors. Grocery shopping was a frightening risk. Six feet apart was not far enough. Isolation was necessary. Still two years away from Craig moving in, I was alone.

Overnight, I'd gone from the *doing* of running two businesses to *being* whether I liked it or not. And I did not like it at all. But at some point, like so many others, I set out to make peace with my powerlessness and anxiety. What was that sound? Wind in the trees? Birdsong ringing where the incessant rush of traffic once owned the airwaves? Nature quickly filled the void, flooding back into the world. The air was cleaner than it had been in decades. The freeway behind my condo that normally echoed with constant noise was empty.

When you can't go wide, the only option is to go deep. The antidote for pandemonium is simplicity. When there is nothing left to do, do nothing. Unintentionally, the government was mandating simplicity, doing one thing at a time—and in my case, paying me for it. As a fitness studio owner, I received grants, no-interest loans, and unemployment. I was being paid to go deep!

Go deep I did. I began to meditate. I practiced being with my fear. I sat in silence or with guidance at least ten minutes a day and often more. I retrained my brain to be less reactive, to pause in each moment to reflect. I learned less to abolish fear and anxiety than to be with it.

One of the scariest parts of COVID is that we would not be able to breathe. So, I got intimate with my breath. I used my breath to guide me to calm. Extending my exhales, I calmed my anxiety. My breath became my anti-anxiety medication. Meditation is my medication. I ultimately found a way to live with all the misinformation and loss of control simply by paying attention to my breath.

The virus threatened, above all else, to take our breath away. Gyrokinesis and Gyrotonic offered a way to deepen our breath, strengthen our lungs, and ultimately, calm down. I followed a dancer and Gyrotonic master trainer based in New York who'd contracted COVID-19 in the early days. I knew her to be reliable, and her experience was tangible. Her videos were the closest I came to the virus directly. In a weak, breathy voice, she talked about her daily struggle to breathe, and how the gentle breathing exercises and heart-opening stretches of Gyrokinesis were saving her.

A year or so later, I took a certification course with her. During one of the breaks, I told her I'd followed her story.

"COVID changed me," she said. "I am not the same person. It softened me."

I wasn't altogether sure she meant this as a good thing. But there was nothing of the exacting, sometimes harsh woman everyone had warned me about. She was soft and kind—if somewhat distant—as though she'd been stripped of the will to try to bend people to her standards. She presented herself like a woman who knew what mattered and had no energy for anything that didn't.

If we're lucky, coming close to death strips us of artifice, perfectionism, and ego. If we're even luckier, we don't have to come close to death to learn to let go of the characteristics that keep us from connection with others.

When COVID finally took me, it didn't come through the door I'd been anticipating. There was no sore throat. Not even a sniffle. It didn't come through the window of a cold or the door of the flu.

While COVID did not affect my lungs, anxiety, another neurological symptom of COVID, also causes shortness of breath. Mindful breathing saved me. I doubled down on my meditation, lying on the floor to ground myself and using box breathing—in-two-three-four, hold-two-three-four, exhale-two-three-four, hold-two-three-four—to pull myself back from the brink of panic attacks.

My experience with the illness changed me too. But what changed me was far bigger than my own bout with a serious illness. What changed me the most were the restrictions on our outer world, the ones that provided a gift and an opportunity. It challenged me to figure out what really matters; it has emboldened me to stand up for my self-care in the most radical way, to investigate the truth, to feel my fragility so I can become stronger and more resilient, to face death so I can be fully, gratefully alive, to appreciate every breath I take as if it's my first—and my last.

WHAT I LEARNED

> "Quiet the mind and the soul will speak."
>
> — Ma Jaya Satt Bhagavati

As my outer world shrank, my inner world expanded. I am not here to debate conspiracy theories or science. This chapter is an exploration of how the past four years affected me—and I believe many of us. It's about how the stay-at-home orders, fear, and confusion forced me into a mindfulness practice that saved my life and opened my soul to others' voices.

This period of pandemonium brought many of us face to face with darkness, mortality, and loneliness. One of my coaching clients, a surgeon, called his first bout with COVID, "The dark night of the soul." It brought him face-to-face with his need for belonging and companionship. For me, it was an opportunity and, ultimately, a test of my mindfulness meditation practice. The thing that threatened to take my breath away invited me to practice breathing.

Aside from the fear and death this period called COVID-19 brought, it gave many of us the gift of silence, of slowing down, of doing one thing at a time. And, as the world came back online, there was a secondary invitation: to be intentional and mindful about what we would allow back into our lives. Many of us refused to go back to work in the same way, either choosing to work at home, change careers, or just take a big, long break.

Of course, frontline workers did not have this luxury—like the surgeon-client I mentioned above. It was the illness itself that ultimately forced him to face his shadows and claim his self-care in a way he never had before. Indeed, he joined other physicians and nurses who realized on a whole new level they had to take care of themselves if they were to sustain a life of service.

SELF-CARE EXERCISES

1. What did you learn about yourself during the pandemic—either by external rules or internal precautions/fears? What gifts did this time give?

   _____

   _____

   _____

   _____

   _____

   _____

1. Reflect on a time when you transformed your fear into something else. How did you use the experience of fear or powerlessness to educate yourself or help others?

   _____

   _____

   _____

   _____

   _____

   _____

1. How do you or can you quiet your mind? Make a list. Make a commitment.

　_____
　_____
　_____
　_____
　_____
　_____
　_____

2. What have you stood up for in your self-care? Where and when do you not stand up for your self-care?

　_____
　_____
　_____
　_____
　_____
　_____
　_____

3. How, if at all, did the past four years help you learn what really matters? How have you protected those values since then?

_____
_____
_____
_____
_____
_____
_____

TIPS FOR BREATHING THROUGH PANDEMONIUM

1. Breathe. Start with counting your breaths, in and out. This is the basis of mindfulness.

2. Ground yourself. If you're anxious or scared, literally get on the floor. Lie down, feel the support of the floor and breathe.

3. If you feel powerless, good. This is the beginning of change. Be with that.

SUMMARY

> "Mindfulness not only makes it possible to survey our internal landscape with compassion and curiosity but can also actively steer us in the right direction for self-care."
>
> — Bessel Van Der Kolk

Healing is an inside job. The stay-at-home orders provided me with an opportunity to go deep and practice mindfulness meditation. At the same time, police murdered a man named George Floyd just a mile from my house. The cry on the streets was echoing Floyd's last words: "I can't breathe." In an instant, what might be labeled "political" became personal. Along with my neighbors and others across the globe, I was compelled to get out of myself and figure out what I stand for. This event changed our city and the world and forced me out of my shrunken world, into the streets to make a stand against racial injustice. It's long been shown that altruism correlates with well-being. Caring about the plight of others and acting on their behalf helps us break free of our own fears and self-pity. Love is stronger than fear. But we must choose it. That's what I did.

It's one thing to come home to yourself. It's another to come home to others. I have done both. I have found deep peace with my children, grandchildren, Craig, and my little dog. I challenge you to dig up your darkness and face it, not just to ask for, but demand, what you need. I challenge you to get beyond performance, not only to show but feel love and compassion where perhaps you haven't before. I challenge you to face your loneliness and embrace your need for belonging. I challenge you to feel your fragility so you can be strong and resilient. I challenge you to face your fear of death, or at least accept it, so you can be fully, gratefully alive. I challenge you to recognize your privilege, to appreciate every breath you take as if it's your first, and your last.

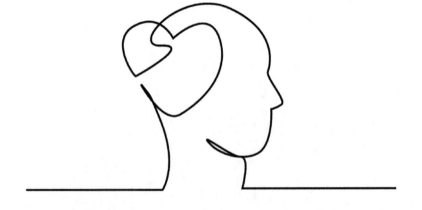

A FINAL NOTE

MANIFESTING YOUR BEST SELF

> "Self-care is giving the world the best of you, instead of what's left of you."
>
> — Katie Reed

It's one thing to read a book—and even do the exercises after each chapter. It's another thing to make it real. Not just today, but day after day. This is the manifesting part. This is the part where you actually change from the inside out. This is about the big idea of habits—a word that makes many of us groan under its weightiness—and for some contains the sense of failure. So many of us think "discipline" when we hear the word "habit." And when we think discipline, we think along the lines of diets, e.g., deprivation. But hear me out.

Creating lasting healthy habits is not the work of deprivation. It is the work of abundance.

Nothing good comes from deprivation. Discipline is built from passion, from love. You repeat behavior not because it's "good for you" or "because you should." You do things again and again because it somehow feels good. Self-disgust might initially drive you to eat better and exercise, but that is not lasting motivation. It is unsustainable. Healthy habits are made of enjoyment and pleasure. But if you do not believe you are worthy of enjoyment, pleasure, happiness, and joy, guess what? You will not indulge in healthy, feel-good activities. And you will not build habits of self-care.

It starts with love. To love yourself even when—especially when—you are unhappy with your body or your "lack of discipline" is the biggest challenge of all. I challenge you to fall in love with yourself. If love is too strong a word for your next step in self-care, start with just getting to know yourself. I challenge you to embark on this journey of self-discovery without judgment. Bring big curiosity. Who is this person who lives inside your skin? My great hope is this book has jump-started your journey of self-discovery. So, now what? What activities, mindset, seminars, and self-care practices will you commit to?

Before you close this book, use the ten lines below to make a commitment to yourself. List ten actions you can take in the next ninety days to create a new blueprint for self-care as the result of reading this book:

1. _____
2. _____
3. _____
4. _____
5. _____
6. _____
7. _____
8. _____
9. _____
10. _____

In this book, you learned the *true* meaning of self-care. Through stories and self-discovery exercises, you uncovered the fundamental tenets of self-care. You learned to transform your trauma, discover the leader within, survive the wildernesses of your life, turn judgment into compassion, and love unconditionally—starting with you. You have worked through the questions in this book in the spirit of an explorer, applying the discovery of what self-care can mean for *you*.

You have begun to apply my Five Wellness Strategies:

1. Set healthy boundaries.
2. Monitor and marshal your energy sources.
3. Create pockets of silence and stillness so you can….
4. Learn the language of your body.
5. Listen to all of yourself: body, heart, mind, spirit, and emotion.

But how do you integrate these strategies so you can fulfill the promise of this book's title? How can you fold these discoveries and preliminary practices into the core of who you are? If you continue to make this book a trusted companion, returning to it again and again, you will come home to your soul's purpose and live the extraordinary life your meant to lead. If you work through this book with the spirit of an explorer, with the goal of finding unconditional friendship with yourself, you will discover the key to living authentically. If you apply the principles, ideas, and strategies in this book, you will finally learn how to put yourself first as the ultimate act of generosity.

Here is where coaching comes in. I founded Wild Hart Coaching LLC (www.WildHartCoaching.com) to help people find their own true and natural hearts so they can achieve the life of freedom, purpose and joy. As a life coach specializing in self-care, I encourage you to reach out to me. Tell me about your challenges, internal gremlins, and greatest strengths so I can help you amplify what's working and diminish what's in your way. You have all the answers within you. Life coaching helps you discover what lays hidden in your heart and soul. I love doing complimentary coaching sessions with no strings attached. In fact, one of the most fulfilling parts of my life is helping people move the needle in a single session.

You can hop on my schedule here:

https://WildHartSchedule.as.me/ComplimentaryCoachingSession.

Or call, email, or text me with your time zone to schedule a complimentary chemistry session:

susan@wildhartcoaching.com

(612) 203-9619

Let's face it, sometimes life can be tough. I challenge you to be tougher. Your days of anxiety, stress, chaos, and fatigue are over. Your days of pouring from an empty cup are done. You've got this. Your best days are yet to come. I believe in you.

Thank you for taking the time and showing the courage to try something new, to apply the wisdom of someone who has walked the path of trauma, healing, and hope. I wish you a life of compassion, joy, and courage!

Your Self-Care Coach,

Susan Hart Gaines

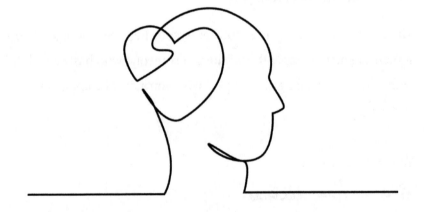

ABOUT THE AUTHOR

SUSAN HART GAINES is an author, keynote speaker, entrepreneur, and certified professional life coach, specializing in helping people of all ages and backgrounds prioritize their self-care. She first discovered her passion for writing when she was in grade school, later achieving her master's degree in journalism from Northwestern University. For several years, Susan had a monthly column with a Twin Cities magazine, where she reported and wrote about health, wellness, and fitness. Her personal stories, written with humility, curiosity, and wisdom, leant inspirational power to her reporting. Spurred by the belief that "We're only as sick as our secrets," Susan's goal has always been to help readers feel less alone, to see their shared humanity.

Susan's column led her to the Gyrotonic® method, first as a journalist and then as a devoted student of this circular, three-dimensional exercise system that helps open the joints, lengthen the muscles, and balance multiple systems of energy in the body. Her personal experience with the transformative power of the Gyrotonic system, created by Juliu Horvath, a Romanian dancer, inspired her to open a studio, which she operates to this day. Through these gentle, rhythmic movements, Susan experienced how we can heal the mind through the body. Her once poor posture became naturally upright, her shoulders and chest opened, and she became more trusting and hopeful. She opened Embody Minneapolis with the strong belief that to become embodied is to become whole and fully alive.

While Susan continued to share her experience, strength, and hope with her Gyrotonic clients, she wanted more tools to help people transform. In 2018, she embarked on the Co-Active® Training Institute's (CTI) life coach training and certification path. She founded her second business, Wild Hart Coaching, where she has helped countless men and women of all ages, from Australia to Africa, control their shame, own their power, and take care of themselves in the deepest ways possible. As a life coach, Susan combines the wisdom of her years of working with bodies and energy pathways with the gold standard CTI model for life coaching. She has earned a reputation among physicians, lawyers, CEOs, stay-at-home parents, and retirees as a warm, courageous, intuitive, and transformative life coach.

Born and raised in Berkeley, California, Susan received her Bachelor of Arts from the University of California, Santa Cruz, where she met her first husband, whom she is friends with to this day. They moved to Chicago, where she attended graduate school, and then Albuquerque, where she first learned that places have power, and no matter how hard we try, we may not have control over what happens next. She and her life partner Craig live with their ten-pound rescue dog named Paxton. Her children and grandchildren live nearby, and she is grateful every day for her membership in a family she would choose again and again—even if they weren't related by blood.

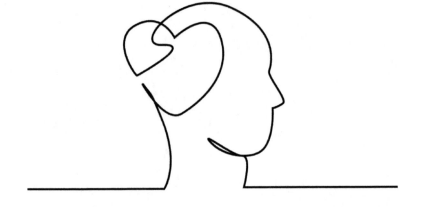

SUSAN HART GAINES SPEAKING AND COACHING

If you are looking for a heart-centered, courageous, articulate, and wise speaker to connect with your audience, look no further than Susan Hart Gaines. Whether your audience is intimate or large, Susan has a way of connecting to each and every person in the room. She is passionate about all things self-care—including boundary-setting, saying No, saying Yes, and knowing your values.

Susan always has a spot or two open for clients looking to shed their negative belief system and practice radical self-care, so they can live with freedom, connection, and success.

For more information on booking Susan for a speaking engagement or coaching, you can learn more and contact her in any of the ways below.

SusanHartGaines.com
www.WildHartCoaching.com
susan@wildhartcoaching.com
(612) 203-9619

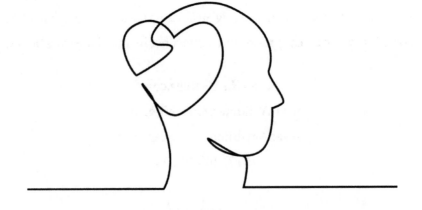

NOTES:

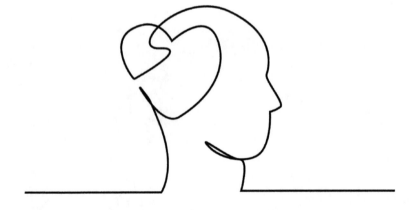

NOTES:

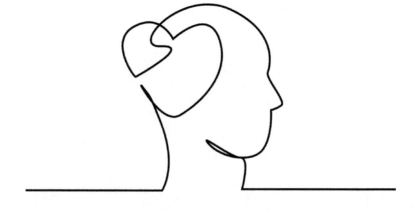

NOTES:

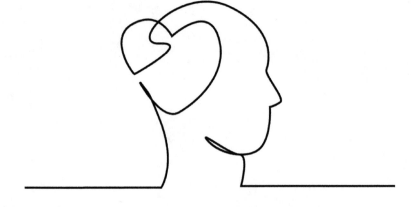